Military Institution in Iran
Between Revolution and Statehood

Editors
Mohammed Saqr Alsulami
&
Fathi Abu Bakr Almaraghy

PARTRIDGE

RASANAH
المعهد الدولي للدراسات الإيرانية
International Institute for Iranian Studies

ISBN: Hardcover   978-1-5437-5847-4
            Softcover   978-1-5437-5845-0
            eBook   978-1-5437-5846-7

To order additional copies of this book, contact
Toll Free +65 3165 7531 (Singapore)
Toll Free +60 3 3099 4412 (Malaysia)
orders.singapore@partridgepublishing.com

www.partridgepublishing.com/singapore

Contents

Introduction

The Iranian military institution is a major player in the Iranian political system and is influenced by the regime's internal and external interactions. At the beginning of the third millennium, the Iranian regime adopted developmental tendencies that marked the end of the Reformist era, the rise of the populist current, and the rise of the moderate current with its inconsistent tendencies as well as those of the Supreme Leadership institution. These events motivated the Iranian military institution to assume a significant internal role that exceeded its basic military responsibility of thwarting external threats. Initially, after the 1979 revolution, the Iranian military institution was tasked with protecting the revolution and its gains, ensuring cultural and social changes that increased the regime's popularity and defeating the regime's enemies in the Iranian political arena.

The Middle East, like Iran, witnessed dramatic changes as well. Over the past two decades, the region saw the fall of Saddam Hussein in Iraq and the Taliban regime in Afghanistan. This led the armed forces of Iran and the United States to come into contact with one another. After this, the region witnessed the Arab Spring revolutions in 2011, the outbreak of the Syrian revolution, and the rise of ISIS, with all its security and military consequences.

In 2015, Iran signed the nuclear deal with the P1+5 group, giving Tehran the opportunity to reintegrate into the international community, as viewed by former US President Barack Obama. He expected Iran to give up its antagonistic policies because of the post-nuclear-deal sanction relief, as well as to normalize relations with neighboring countries and improve cooperation with the international community. However, Iran adopted more antagonistic policies than it maintained before. It involved itself in armed conflicts in the region by sending its troops to Syria and forming hundreds of proxy militias from among the Shiite minorities in Pakistan, Afghanistan, Iraq, Lebanon, and Syria. Indeed, the Iranian military institution led and directed these proxy militias on the ground outside its borders and directed its regular forces in the adoption of asymmetrical warfare strategies.

The change in Iran's military role and its practices led to a heated argument among all Iranian political currents about its limits, ideology, and combat doctrine, as well as the constitutional rules organizing the military and its compliance with the Iranian political system, both internally and externally. In addition, every so often a hidden dispute between the Iranian regular army and the IRGC takes a political shape because of the IRGC's expansionist inclinations and the extension of its economic empire. These developments highlight the important role of the Iranian military institution and the need to study this institution forty years after the 1979 revolution. Such an effort will reveal facts and answer questions relating to the Iranian military institution between the state and the revolution.

On May 2014,14, the International Institute for Iranian Studies (formerly known as the Arabian Gulf Center for Iranian Studies) held a workshop titled, "The Iranian Military Institution between the State and Revolution" in Riyadh, the capital city of the Kingdom of Saudi Arabia. The workshop's goal was to understand the "Other" and its capabilities, as well as its points of strength and weakness and its direct and indirect tools. The workshop analyzed three central aspects of the Iranian military institution: its ideological dimension and military doctrine, its role in the balance of political power, and its involvement in the outside world. The research papers in this book are the result of lengthy discussions and the exchange of ideas among Iranian affairs specialists – both participants and nonparticipants in the workshop – over the course of a year, until the publication of this book.

The papers in this book are arranged so that they shift from the general to the particular as follows:

» The Ideological Dimension of the Military Institution by Sultan Mohammad Alnuaimi (Ph.D.). In this study, the writer handles the ideology of the Iranian military institution by analyzing how through its ideological and moral guidance institutions, the military promotes its ideology among its personnel, as well as to all social segments in Iran.

» The Relationship between the Military Institution and the Iranian Political System in Light of Compatibility Theory by Fathi Abu Bakr Almaraghy (Ph.D.). In this study, the writer discusses the theories explaining the nature of relations between the Iranian military institution and the political system. The writer explains concepts related to the Iranian regime and military institution in terms of their structure, rise, and role. The writer measures the consensus level among them by analyzing four facets: the social composition of military personnel, the political decision-making process of the military institution, the recruitment channels, and the pattern in which the military institution evaluates public views and values towards itself.

» The Military Doctrine of the Iranian Armed Forces: Considering the Dual Army and the Revolutionary Guards by Mo'taz Mohammad Salama. In this study, the writer presents a new view of what he calls "Basdarat" – the Iranian social and state doctrine. This means the IRGC has integrated itself into the center of the state and imposed its ideology and military doctrine on society and the army. The writer handles the external expansionist tendency in the IRGC doctrine, such as pre-emptive wars, carving out spheres of influence, flaring sectarian wars, cloning the IRGC, guerrilla warfare, and promoting terrorism. The writer concludes his study by devising a strategy for breaking down the IRGC military doctrine and promoting gradual change in Iran by de-militarizing society while maintaining a strategy of nonmilitary confrontation with the IRGC doctrine and introducing a new model of development by the GCC countries, with the goal of embarrassing the Iranian regime in front of its own people.

» The Iranian Military Institution: Combat Capabilities, Deployment Plans, and Functions by Saad Mohammad Ibn Nami (Ph.D.). In this study, the writer presents a statistical view of Iranian military capabilities and the military industry. He offers a comprehensive explanation of the deployment of Iranian ground, naval, and air forces, as well as an analysis of the Iranian electronic warfare units and cyber army.

» Militarization of Shiism by Mohammed Saqr Alsulami (Ph.D.), Chairman of the International Institute for Iranian Studies. In this study, the writer presents his view of the concept of "militarizing Shiism." Firstly, the writer handles militarization as an independent variable and Shiism as a dependent variable. Secondly, he handles Shiism as an independent variable and militarization as a dependent variable. In addition, the writer handles militarizing Shiism inside and outside Iranian borders by discussing two factors: the impact of Shiism on the IRGC and the impact of militarization on Shiism.

» An Assessment of the Iranian Military Doctrine and Military Leadership: Developments, Obstacles, and Prospects for Change by Alex Vatanka (Ph.D.). In this study, the writer discusses the consolidation of the doctrine of asymmetric warfare in the Iranian military institution, the concept of the Martyr State, the change in Iranian military tactics after a change in the nature of the enemy in the Iranian mentality, and the role of Iran's partners in supporting the Iranian military institution.

» The Economic Activities of the Iranian Revolutionary Guards Corps (IRGC): Tools and Implications on Iran and the Region by Ahmad Shamsuddin Leila. In this study, the writer handles the economic activities of the IRGC and their internal and external impact by discussing several facets, such as the tools supporting the IRGC's economic strength. The IRGC controls a significant part of the Iranian banking sector, the Iranian borders that facilitate its smuggling activities, and the Iranian Bazaar. Externally, the IRGC uses its external military operations to establish economic agreements for political purposes with countries like Iraq. Also, it carries out reconstruction projects in the countries where IRGC elements reside.

The Ideological Dimension of the Military Institution

Sultan Mohammad Alnuaimi (Ph.D.)
Associate Professor of Iranian Studies at Abu Dhabi University

The religious, ideological dimensions of Shiite sectarianism, especially the Twelvers, was a significant advantage for the post1979- revolution Iranian regime. This was clearly visible in the preamble to the Constitution, which mentioned that the main advantage of this revolution over others in Iran during the last century was the sectarian revolution and Islamism.[1] The Islamization of the regimes' institutions was a major goal of the religious current to fortify its existence and remove other forces involved in the revolution (the liberal and left currents).

The religious current took advantage of Iran's prevailing religious tendencies. A number of religious thoughts and ideas had penetrated society, particularly the thoughts of the Iranian intellectual Ali Shariati, * who sparked Shiite revolutionary inclinations. He devoted himself to restoring the concepts of Islamic Shiism as they were in the period of Imam Ali Ibn Abi Talib—may God bless him. Shariati drew a comparison between "Alawis Shiism," referring to Ali Ibn Abi Talib and "Safavid Shiism" referring to the Safavid state. He viewed the Safavid state as having monopolized religious belief and isolating the Shiite sect from political and social affairs. The Safavids thought that the Twelfth Imam required the Shiites to wait until his return and refrain from participating in political affairs. However, Shariati claimed that "Alawis Shiism" represented the true picture of the Shiite religion, which called for both a fair society and for believers to take control of their own affairs. He dealt with the concept of the absent Imam, which he believed should not be a cause for Taqiyya and self-absorption, but rather an invitation for Muslims to take responsibility for their own affairs under a religious and enlightened leadership which can help them raise awareness and realize their aspirations.[2]

Thanks to Khomeini and his charisma, the religious, ideological dimension began to take shape. Khomeini insisted on describing the 1979 revolution as an Islamic revolution: "We set off revolution for the sake of Islam, and our martyrs sacrificed themselves for Islam and nothing else."[3] This description of the revolution gradually and deliberately became a means to consolidate the authority of religious currents and remove liberal and leftist thoughts from governance. This religious alignment was seen in the military institutions in Iran, such as in the regular army and the Revolutionary Guard; the sectarian political commission played a significant role in indoctrinating the personnel to ensure their loyalty to the regime and the political system.

The Military Institution and the Constitution

After the Shah's period, the Islamic regime infiltrated existing institutions and developed others to serve its ideology, such as the *Majlis Melli* (Parliament), which later became known as the Islamic Consultative Assembly (Shura Islamic

Council). This was all in accordance with the Constitution, which was written to give the Supreme Leader authority and legitimacy since he is the deputy of the absent Imam. The Constitution emphasized the importance of Iran's military institutions and gave a clear perspective of their ideology. The preamble to the Constitution states.

In the field of building and equipping the country's armed forces; the primary concern is to make faith and religion a priority. Thus, these forces are not only responsible for protecting and guarding the borders, but also for the divine mission, the jihad for the sake of Allah, and the jihad for the extension of the rule of the divine law.[4]

Article 144 of the Constitution states, "The Army of the Islamic Republic of Iran must be an Islamic army, i.e. committed to Islamic ideology and the people. It must accept into its service deserving individuals who are true to the goals of the Islamic Revolution and devoted to realizing them."[5] The sectarian political commission came to play a role in promoting the ideological dimension of the revolution and motivating the regime to transfer the revolution beyond its borders. We will highlight the Revolutionary Guard extensively because it is the pillar of the regime in maintaining its survival and continuity, and clearly reflects the ideological dimension of the revolution. The current Supreme leader Khamenei described the Revolutionary Guard and its difference from other forces such as the regular army:

The army remains like the Revolutionary Guard, but I believe that the only force capable of defending the revolution, the regime of the Islamic Republic and the revolutionary defense is the Revolutionary Guards… if we do not have or weak revolutionary forces, we will not be able to defend the revolution. We must reinforce the true meaning of the word 'Revolutionary Guard' and then the moral dimensional aspects such as spirit, intellect, faith, sincerity and other aspects which distinguish the Revolutionary Guard from the rest of the armed forces. If not, the Revolutionary Guard has no meaning.[6]

In another statement, Khamenei said,

«Today, the Iranian army is honorable and has public support. Our security and police forces have exceptional positions compared to their counterparts in the world, but the Revolutionary Guard has the distinctiveness of having grown in the middle of the revolution. Therefore, if the others became revolutionaries, the Revolutionary Guard was created as revolutionary.»[7]

The ideological dimension of the Revolutionary Guards

According to the Revolutionary Guard's regulations, which were ratified by the Iranian Parliament on September 1982,6, article 1 of Chapter 1 states,

> The Revolutionary Guard is an Islamic institution under the Supreme Leader, whose goal is to protect the Iranian Islamic Revolution and its achievements and make continuous effort to protect the divine goals. The extension of the divine law of the Islamic Republic of Iran and the reinforcement of the other defense structures of the Islamic Republic come through cooperation with the other armed forces and the institutions of public force.[8]

In addition, Article 15 gives the Commander-in-Chief of the Revolutionary Guard responsibility over all the Basij forces, which are the smallest unit in the Revolutionary Guard. Their curricula and educational programmes are sectarian and politically driven.

The sectarian political commission was established to determine the sectarian and political curriculum for the Revolutionary Guard's members, as well as to establish the advertising and publishing units to write and publish books, magazines, and bulletins, as long as all the publications were approved by the Supreme Leader or his representative.[9] To strengthen the Revolutionary Guard's sectarian and ideological dimension, offices of the representatives of the Supreme Leader exist to supervise the Revolutionary Guard and to help the Supreme Leader carry out his duties. The appointment or removal of Revolutionary Guard officials comes through the representatives of the Supreme Leader. These offices consist of a supervisory office responsible for supervising the Revolutionary Guard and preparing reports for the representatives of the Supreme Leader, and a political office responsible for gathering and analyzing news and political events. As the main purpose of the Revolutionary Guard is to defend the revolution and its achievements, the conditions for membership reflect this objective. According to Article 34 of the Revolutionary Guards' regulation, the term "the guardian (Pâsdâr)" refers to a person who has been trained in a Revolutionary Guard institution; even if he moves to another governmental institute, he will still have the status of "guardian." The following conditions must be fulfilled by those who wish to join the Revolutionary Guard or the Basij:

1. Belief in Islamic principles, the Islamic revolution, and the Islamic republic regime.
2. Faith and practical commitment to the Supreme Leader.

3. A practical commitment to the provisions of Islam and the laws of the Islamic Republic.
4. Does not belong to any political party or organization.
5. Good conduct.

Article 47 reaffirms the Revolutionary Guard's subordination, both political and sectarian, to the Supreme Leadership, and its independence from any political parties or organizations. Accordingly, under Article 48, members of the Revolutionary Guard are not allowed to belong to any party or political organization. Khomeini stated that the Iranian Revolutionary Guard should not participate in political life; this is the opposition's evidence for refusing the Revolutionary Guard any interference in the political arena. Despite this idea, the Revolutionary Guard's duty of protecting the revolution and its achievements has moved to political and cultural areas. However, a representative of the Supreme Leader has justified the Revolutionary Guard's "election engineering." Likewise, the Ministry of Logistics Support for Defense and Armed Forces published an article titled "Political Questions and Answers" on its website. The typical answer to the question as to why the Revolutionary Guard Commanders intervened in politics, contrary to what Khomeini said, was as follows:

«The statement of His Holiness [Khomeini] regarding the prohibition of the armed forces intervening in politics indicates that members of the armed forces belong to political parties, or are aligned to a political party at another one's expense. As for the activities of the Revolutionary Guard, if a political group operating within the country calls for the separation of religion from politics, or if there is a political party that favors the granting of special privileges to a foreign government, the Revolutionary Guard considers itself obliged to object and to publish its objection to the public because the Supreme Leader, the ideal leader, and the integrity of the homeland has been attacked. Such matters are not considered intervention; they are within the responsibility of the IRGC.»[10]

This analysis would not be far away from the perspective of the current Supreme Leader, who sees the revolutionary army as a military organization with political and cultural inclinations: "I'm not saying here that it is a military-political or military-cultural organization, that's another thing. The tendencies of this military group are mixed with the political alignment and more importantly the cultural alignment."[11]

Regarding training courses focusing on the ideological dimension, Iranian researcher Ali Founa, in his study titled "Indoctrination of the Revolutionary Guard," found that educational centers for the Revolutionary Guard host training courses and sessions. The Martyr Mahlalti University, established in 1982 and formerly known as the University of Islamic Science and Culture, was the most advanced center for training and politically indoctrinating the Revolutionary Guard. Assigning the Martyr Mahlalti University's graduates indoctrination tasks grants the Revolutionary Guard the privilege to supervise itself without censorship.[12] On the importance of the sectarian political commission's role in the Revolutionary Guard, Brigadier General Muhammad Hussein Sabhar, an Assistant Representative of the Supreme Leader of the Revolutionary Guard said:

«From the beginning of the guard's formation, its main assets were: faith, spirituality, religious and political insight, faith in the Supreme Leadership, and revolutionary motivation… which made the Revolutionary Guard the center of hope for revolutionaries throughout the Islamic world… This commission has become strategic and operational in the fields of training and development. An impressive number of annual programs have been devoted to educational, ideological and political issues that have led to the satisfaction of the representative for the superior performance of the Guard.»[13]

The job of the sectarian political commission does not stop at that point,* but also involves developing the curricula and materials to deepen the sectarian dimension of the Revolutionary Guard to make it more committed to the revolutionary thought and the protection of the system. During the previous period, several developmental steps were taken, as follows:

» Production of texts to cover the need for political, cultural and sectarian activities with the Islamic Studies Research Institute "Imam Sadiq" in Qom. A large number of researchers in this Institute carry out this task and assess demand throughout the year.

» Training, educating and benefiting from the political and sectarian trainers at the Martyr Mahlalti University campus, the majority of them are clerks, and they are advocates of the sectarian political commission.

» Attracting, training and organizing the network of political mentors for the Revolutionary Guard and its mobilizers, providing an extensive network of a thousand mentors across Iran to meet many of the needs of the Revolutionary Guard and its mobilizers in the political guidance section, while benefiting from the political and elite mentors in the Hawza and the University.[14]

In endorsing the sectarian dimension, the Revolutionary Guard does not confine sectarian courses to its members only, but also invites families and relatives, after agreement between the Commander-in-Chief of the Revolutionary Guard and the representative of the Supreme Leader to send members of the Revolutionary Guard with their families to participate in training and development courses in the cities of Qom and Mashhad.

Brigadier General Hussein Zarif Mansh, the Commander of the Imam Hussein Academy, introduced a new aspect of the ideological dimension of the Revolutionary Guard by saying, "The Revolutionary Guards can play a big role in the Islamization of human sciences in universities." This statement came after the invitation of the Supreme Leader Ali Khamenei to have the Islamic dimension included in those sciences, after the events of 2009 and the large participation of university youth. The leaders of the Revolutionary Guard were not only convinced of guiding universitiesremotely, butthey alsodecidedto establishuniversities in the provinces that would accept members of the Revolutionary Guard and even recruits and educate students in specific topics. This recent plan of the Revolutionary Guard was managed for years by the administrations of Imam Hussein University, the Medical University of Bakhitullah, the Training Center for Ideology and Politics in Qom, and the Martyr Mahlalti University. The Revolutionary Guard established higher educational centers throughout the country, which was highlighted by Colonel Behrouz Shahb, the Head of the Higher Education Center Imam Hussein in Tehran, during an interview with the weekly newspaper officially affiliated with the Revolutionary Guard *Sobh Sadiq*.[15] Surely, the ideological dimension of the Revolutionary Guard plays a major role in the ideology of the regime by continuing the revolution as the basis for the regime's continuation. As a result, the demand for ending the revolutionary features in Iran is strongly criticized by the Supreme Leader and the leaders of the Revolutionary Guard. During the Supreme Leader's meetings, whether with the Council of Experts or with the members of the Supreme National Security Council, he has always focused on the need for continuing the revolution, and has even demanded that the choice of his successor match his revolutionary methodological beliefs. The Commander of the Revolutionary Guard, Mohammed Ja'fari, said:

There is no meaning of the Islamic Republic without the Islamic revolution and its continuation. On the other hand, opponents of the revolution claim that as long as the Islamic regime has stabilized, there is no need for the continuation of the revolution and the task of consolidating the revolution internally and externally has been entrusted to the Guard and the Basij by the Supreme Leader's decision; therefore, it is wrong to claim that the role of guards and Basij are limited to natural borders only.[16]

Considering the ideological dimension and its importance in the Revolutionary Guard, the Supreme Leader Khamenei believes that, in addition to military education and exercises, religious, faith and sectarian education is the most important thing for Revolutionary Guard members to have; the representative of the Supreme Leader in the Revolutionary Guard is responsible for this. According to Khamenei, the Revolutionary Guard must have a moral connection with leadership and the Supreme Leadership.[17] To link the thought of the Revolutionary Guard with Shiite sectarianism and its continuity, Khamenei demands that the theme of all Revolutionary Guard members is "I am a Guardian, following the footsteps of Hussain Ibn Ali" and he emphasizes that "the necessity of following the correct path, preserving the moral aspects and the values of our master Hussein is an integral part of the duties of the Revolutionary Guards."[18]

In fact, Khamenei's vision completes Khomeini's vision, which was to have the Revolutionary Guard entrusted with protecting the revolution. Ayatollah Khomeini's statements at the beginning of the revolution had much significance for military institutions and their ideological dimensions. Khomeini described the Revolutionary Guard as soldiers at the beginning of Islam and gave them a major role in the protection of the Islamic revolution and in the rise of Islam.[19] Khomeini's vision of protecting the revolution was not limited to protecting Iran's borders; he addressed the Revolutionary Guards, "Today you are in an Islamic state, and you live under Islam, and you are his guards. Guardianship is not only the protection of borders, but it also has wider meanings."[20] This emphasized the ideological dimension of the Revolutionary Guard as going beyond the protection of borders. General Commander of the Revolutionary Guard, Major General Mohammed Jafari, likewise said, "Initially, the guard was not supposed to be a military, it became imperative for the guards to enter these fields, but we must not forget that the philosophy of the guards' is to maintain order and the successes of the revolution." He reiterated this by saying,

There is no doubt that the foreign attack threatens the people's security and territorial integrity, but the Islamic revolution today faces greater challenges with the existence of political, cultural and economic threats...... Here lies the self-task of the Guard, which is to intervene in the event of political, cultural and economic threats that would strike or distort the Islamic revolution.

Then, he criticized those who demanded the Guard's removal from political life by stating "The Revolutionary Guards defend the command of the Supreme Leader and the general directions of the revolution in the political, cultural and social fields, and this defense of the Guard is for the principles and successes of the Islamic Revolution."[21] The Commander of the Revolutionary Guard implements Khomeini's vision, who called for the Revolutionary Guard, in peacetime and in harmony with the principle of a special resolution known as "defense in all aspects," to work until they reach 20 million guards and Basijis.[22]

Khomeini did not miss any chance to speak about the Revolutionary Guard's sectarian dimension: "We are all guardians of the absent Imam, and I hope that as Islam has lived by the sacrifice of Hussein, you (the Revolutionary Guard) will be sacrificing to preserve and guarantee the revolution and Islam."[23] Khomeini constantly strived to link the revolution, the Iranian regime and the Revolutionary Guard, like when he said, "I say unequivocally that the Islamic Revolution, the Islamic Republic, and the Revolutionary Guard institution were truly one of the greatest trenches to defend the divine values of our regime and they will be, and there is a need for each one of you (guards)."[24] Khomeini saw that, the five stages of the revolution are the victory of the revolution, the stability of the Islamic system, the formation of an Islamic government, the building of an Islamic community, and assistance in developing the world community of Islam and we are in the third and fourth stage, undoubtedly the last three stages should progress with each other. Therefore, the Commander-in-Chief Ja'fari believes that it is not possible to focus only on military activities but also on other different fields, and not only in dealing with military aspects.[25]

The continuation of the ideological and the revolutionary dimensions are important to guarantee the continuation of the regime and the revolution and to complete the five stages. Thus, strengthening the ideological dimension of the military institutions will result in the transfer of this ideology to other fields, thereby strengthening the influence of the Iranian regime in the region and impacting peace and stability in the region negatively.

Endnotes

(1) Full text of the Constitution of the Islamic Republic of Iran, 3rd ed., (Dar Huda Cultural and Art of International Publishing, 13,(2012.

(*) Ali Shareati. Ali bin Mohammed Ibn Taghi Shareati was born in Khorasan in 1933. His father, Muhammad Taqi, was one of the most prominent Islamic thinkers and mujahedeen. With other clerics, he founded the Islamic Truth Center in Mashhad and completed his studies in Mashhad. In this early period of his life, he joined the youth wing of the National Front. After the fall of Mossadegh, he joined the resistance movement founded by Zanjani, Talani and Mehdi Bazargan. Then, Shareati was imprisoned for six months and could not graduate from the Faculty of Arts. Despite these circumstances, Shareati was sent on a mission to France after graduating from the Faculty of Arts with a degree of excellence. In 1964, he received a doctorate in sociology from Sorbonne University. When he returned to Iran, he was arrested at the border under the pretext of his participation in political activities while studying in France. In 1965, he began his teaching at the University of Mashhad. As a Muslim sociologist, Shareati wanted to clarify Islamic principles and discuss them with his students. Even if he did not gain great popularity in the university and in the various social classes in Iran, the regime felt danger and fear from him, so the regime decided to stop his classes in the university and transfer him to a primary school. Shareati continued his lectures in the Guidance Husseiniya, which opened in 1969. For the outstanding success of Dr. Shareati's classes, the authorities closed the Guidance Husseiniya in 1973 and arrested many of his followers. Dr. Shareati was then imprisoned for 18 months and tortured. After being released in March 1975, he remained under surveillance, which forced him to go to London, where he was poisoned in June 1977. His important books include: Where to begin, The task of a free thinker, A look at the understanding of Islam, The philosophy of supplication, Alawis Shiism and the Safavid Shiism, He return to self, and others. Shareati is called the Iranian Revolution theorist because of his contribution to mobilizing the feelings of the Iranian people against the Shah (See Fazel Rasoul, As Ali Shareati spoke, 9-7, and Virvand Ibrahimian, Iran between the coup, 574-571).

(2) See: Ali Shareati, Alawis shiism and the Safavid Shiism (Tehran: Ghalam Publication House, 80-78,(1986.

(3) Sapahr, Zabih. The Story of the Iranian Revolution, trans. Abdulwahab, Alloub, 1st Ed. (Cairo: Supreme Council of Culture, 125,(2004.

(4) Full text of the Constitution of the Islamic Republic of Iran, 21.

(5) Ibid., 74.

(6) See: Khamenei. "IRGC born from Revolution," Khamenei's speeches while meeting with IRGC and Basij, Issue 1, prepared by Mohammad, Ghassimi (Tehran: IRGC Public Relations Office, 77-76 (2011.

(7) Ibid., 99.

(8) "IRGC Foundational Statement," Center for Studies and Researches in the Iranian Parliament, http://cutt.us/7XQxX.

(9) Ibid.

(10) See Ali, Founa, "Indoctrination of the Revolutionary Guard," http://cutt.us/Sei4A.

(11) See: "IRGC born from Revolution," 885.

(12) See: Ali, Founa, "Indoctrination the Revolutionary Guard."

(13) "Religious education and political ideology are the core of IRGC," Enghelab News, http://cutt.us/BzsU.

* The Revolutionary Guard camps hold several courses and activities including:

- Educational courses for one week throughout the day in the centers of the provinces, including the cities of Qom and Mashhad, benefiting from expert professors in the estate and the university. This is one of the most important programs of political doctrine in recent years.

- Holding classes of «Noor Mubeen» in order enjoy the Qurьan and understand the meanings of the Qurьan on the first day of each week throughout the Guard Center.

- Holding political meetings on modern issues and responding to political suspicions for all categories of guards.

- Production and distribution of software, books, magazines, publications and political and analytical products for different levels.

- Conducting training workshops, increasing trainers' skills of political analysis and political guides. See: "The talk of the assistant coordinator of the representative of Supreme Leadership in the guard around the general axis of the movement of the representative of the Supreme Leadership," Enghelab News, http://cutt.us/BzsU.

(14) Ibid.

(15) Hamid, Mafi, "The grip of IRGC on educational and academic centers," Radio Zamane, http://cutt.us/IUI4N.

(16) "Injuries of soft war must be known and treated," Mashriq, http://cutt.us/etQOx.

(17) See: "IRGC born from Revolution," 103.

(18) Ibid, 323.

(19) Mohammad, Qassem, "If the IRGC was not: IRGC and the Islamic Revolution in the thought of Khomeini," 1st Vol., 1st Ed., (Tehran: IRGC Public Relations Office, 229,(2012.

(20) Ibid, 301.

(21) Neda, Esfahan, "20 maneuvers will be conducted by army," http://cutt.us/EgcOT.

(22) "If the IRGC was not," 847.

(23) "If the IRGC was not," 436.

(24) Forum of western bloggers, "IRGC from the view point of Khomeini and Khamenei," http://cutt.us/qhgcn.

(25) "Injuries of soft war must be known and treated," Mashriq, http://cutt.us/zB8ij.

The Relationship between the Military Institution and the Iranian Political System in Light of Compatibility Theory

Fathi Abu Bakr Almaraghy (Ph.D.)
Head of Center for Researches and Studies at Rasanah

The relationship between military institutions and the regime represents one of the challenges facing democratic systems in modern times. Contemporary political principles require that the civil government controls the military institution to ensure the integrity of democratic practices and the stability of country and society. However, these principles suggest an interactive relationship and supportive role that the military institution plays with respect to the civil authority – in some cases, to consolidate the safety of political life. In the case of revolutionary countries or those that derive the regime's legitimacy from ideological legitimacy, the relationship between the military institution and the political authority becomes more closely related to the extent of the military's participation in the revolutionary work that led to the establishment of the regime, as well as to the natures, compositions, and roles of the political system and the military institution.

Political theories about the relationship between the military institution and the political system

Many political theories focus on the nature of the relationship between the military institution and the civil authority because of this relationship's importance in directing the processes of the democratic transformation and institutional development of the state, as well as of the transition from the stages of revolution and military coup to the stage of the civil state. These theories are as follows:

Separation Theory

This theory is based on the idea of the professionalism of the military institution as presented by Samuel Huntington[1] and completed by Harold Trinkunas. The theory stems from the military's separation, ideologically and physically, from the country's political institutions. The belief is that the separation of the professional military from politics leaves no room for interference in civil policies and institutions. The imposition of such a separation requires the existence of a group of civil institutions that can impose political control over the country's armed forces.[2] The peak of this approach is the appointment of a civil defense minister, as well as a series of other procedures that create the legislative authority or the head of the executive authority controlling the appointments, transfers, salaries, arming the military institution's members and prohibiting them from assuming electoral activities during any official elections.

Theory of Competitiveness and Power Sharing

This theory addresses the inadequacy of other theories in explaining civil authority's inability to control the military institution, especially in newly democratic countries. The theory describes the power that enables civil authority to control the militaryinstitutionbasedontheoutcomeoftheircompetitioninfive decision-making areas: recruiting the elite, making public policy, internal security, national defense, and military organization. civil control can be achieved only through full control of these five areas, while the military can undermine civil authority through special privilege, constitutional immunity, challenges to civil authority, and threats to place direct pressure on the government, which could lead to a military coup that ends civil rule.[3] The success of the military's intervention is supported by both the low popularity of the ruling regime and the decline of civil society activities, with an increasing expectation of external and internal risks. However, civil elites can play a major role in controlling the five areas mentioned above and then strengthening civil control of the military institution.

Concordance Theory

This theory, developed by Rebecca Schiff, is based on the ability of the military institution, political elites, and citizens to compromise and achieve a cooperative relationship among themselves. It is also based on three levels of analyzing the military-civilian relationship – military, political leadership, and citizens – while setting criteria for measuring concordance, as follows:

1. The social composition of the military institution's members by involving all sects and the entire ranks of the people to achieve concordance between the military and the community.
2. The political decision-making process of the military, to increase concordance whenever the decisions made are consistent with the needs and requirements of the military.
3. Recruitment methods; a compulsory recruitment system decreases compatibility, while voluntary recruitment increases it.[4]

Analysis levels of the relationship between civilians and the military

According to concordance theory, the levels of relationship analysis between the military and civilians are divided into three levels according to an organization that aligns with the nature of the democratic systems that keep the military away from civil society and subordinates it to the authority of the political leadership.

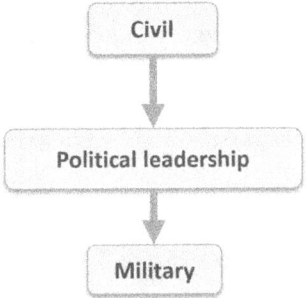

Clarifying which of these three theories can be used to explain the relationship between the military institution and the civil authority in Iran (in other words, the role of the military in Iranian political life) requires consideration of the Iranian military institution and political life or the political system in Iran. Then the relationship between them must be clarified.

While the relationship between civilians and the political and military authorities in democratic systems is hierarchical in nature, we see the Iranian situation influenced by the nature of both the political and the military institutions in Iran, as well as by the position on the political side. Theoretically, people in Iran are not the source of authority and the ruling regime. Specifically, the legitimacy of the current ruling regime is a divine legitimacy, not a public one. The analysis levels of the relationship between civilians and the military in Iran can be viewed as follows:

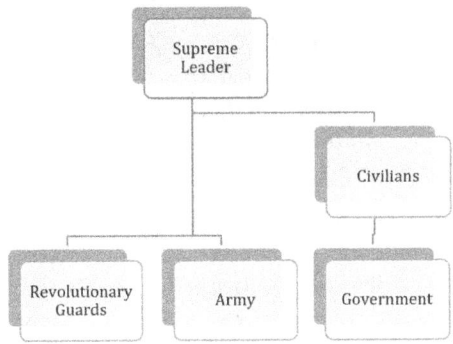

The nature of the political system in Iran

The Iranian regime presents itself as a unique experiment that does not apply to Western democratic regimes. Its name rejects the concept of democracy and employs the term "Mardam Salari Dini," meaning public religious sovereignty instead of democracy. During the drafting of the Iranian Constitution and referendum, Khomeini objected strongly to the addition of the term "democracy" to the country's name and insisted on the Islamic Republic of Iran without adding "democracy" or deleting "Islamic."[5]

Generally, the political system and political life in Iran contains some elements of the democratic system, such as electoral processes, political pluralism, parliamentary representation, and a constitution that forms the basis of the laws governing the country. It also contains elements that go beyond the familiar Western democratic systems, such as the presence of a head of the country who supervises the political system due to him being a deputy of the absent Imam. According to the political- religious belief of Iran, the Supreme Leadership is another deputy of the last Imam of Prophet Muhammad's family. He takes over the political and spiritual authorities and belongs to a specific functional group. The Supreme Leader is chosen by the elite of his functional group (the clergy). He stays in his position forever and establishes the regime's institutions by appointment, apart from the elected authority. He also practices oversight roles on it such as (The Guardian Council that has the right to interpret the Constitution and ratify the decisions of the elected parliament, the appointment of the head of the judiciary, and the appointment of all the military leadership).[6] In addition to asserting his political powers, the Supreme Leader maintains spiritual, religious authority in terms of the right to interpret religious texts, jurisprudence, and fatwa.

In fact, political power in Iran is divided into two institutions. One is the Supreme Leader institution,[7] which is the first pillar of the political authority and which does not permit citizens' participation. Instead, the institution is formed through the selection of the Experts Council.[8] Because a popular referendum is not held to choose the Supreme Leader, he cannot be isolated from power except in rare cases, and he remains unquestioned by parliament. The supreme leader appoints all elements of the Supreme Leader institution who hold positions of a supervisory nature over the elected executive institutions.

The second pillar of political power in Iran is the government or the executive branch, headed by the President of the Republic. It is elected by the people after the practice of the Guardianship Council,[9] the process of selecting candidates taking into account political considerations, primarily without supreme Leader objection. The President of the Republic is not allowed to appoint or remove any of the following Iranian military leaders: the commander of the Revolutionary Guard, the commander of the Iranian army, the commander of the Quds Force, the chief of staff of the armed forces, and the commander of the central base Khatam Anbia. The President of the Republic has the right to determine the budget of the branch of the military institution, but his proposals are often rejected if they do not comply with the guide's desires. This is what happened with Iranian President Hassan Rouhani and the 2017 budget.[10]

The Iranian military institution, formation, growth and role

According to theories in the study of military institutions, the term "military institution" includes all armed organizations within a country, including the police and gendarmerie forces or any armed force whose work is directed toward preserving the integrity of the land and its unity in the face of external aggression or an internal security issue. As for the Iranian situation, the term includes fully armed combat force branches, which the Iranian constitution has given legal permission to in certain cases. We will then focus on the two major factions of the Iranian military institution and IRGC. To begin, we would like to emphasize that there is a significant difference between the army and the Revolutionary Guard in terms of formation, growth, role, and sectarianism.

Formation

a. Army

According to the classification of military entities, the Iranian army is a professional military organization whose primary function is to manage violence and provide necessary services to the community regarding maintaining security and protecting against external dangers. In terms of the theory of separation with respect to the civil relationship and the military, Huntington considers professionalism to be one of the mechanisms that prevents political intervention by the military. In contrast, Samuel Fanner believes that professionalism motivates military intervention in political affairs because it emphasizes separation from society and reinforces the military's awareness of its professional affiliations, which refers to "trade unionism."[11]

b. Revolutionary Guard

The Revolutionary War classification applies to the Iranian Revolutionary Guard Corps because it is a military organization linked to the revolutionary situation and harvesting the objectives of revolution. Therefore, it loses some of its independence and adjusts some of its professional military characteristics for the party or the revolutionary movement. The military organization also becomes the instrument of assembly and mobilization and extends to educational and cultural policy.[12] At the same time, the Iranian Revolutionary Guard can be classified as Praetorianism – a situation in which the military organization uses or threatens to use force to play an independent political role in society. As a result, political institutions within the country – both the political leadership and the political system as a whole – become weak or illegitimate. This increases the military's sense of dominance because of the strength of the military institution, the military's discipline, and the military's sense of privilege over the civil institution and of its own heroic role in protecting the country. Thus, the military intervenes and maximizes its political influence as a means of controlling the political system and political strategy.[13]

Establishment

a. Army

The Iranian army did not participate in the revolution of 1979, announcing the succession of the Islamic republic, or replacing the Shah's regime. The revolutionaries considered the Iranian army to be an instrument of repression used against them and an economic burden that consumed 35% of the country's budget.[14] Despite the diversity of Iranian participants in the revolution, no soldiers joined the revolution, even during the final stages before the fall of the Shah, "with the exception of some air force personnel who rebelled against the Shah and distributed weapons to the rebels." The clerics, led by Ayatollah Khomeini, dominated the political scene. They appointed a transitional civilian government led by Mehdi Bazargan, who was a representative of the National Front Line. Bazargan was a liberal with political experience, which meant that an alliance between national liberal forces and clerics formed during the first year after the revolution, completely excluding the military from political life. Furthermore, the clerics succeeded in issuing the Iranian Constitution, which gave the Supreme Leader the right to supervise political life. It granted him broad political powers and established a number of governing institutions that consolidated the country's clerical control and made them a dominant functional group. During the era of the Republic, the establishment of the Iranian army was based on the stance of factions involved in the revolution from the army. The clerics involved in the revolution did not trust the Iranian army, so subjugating this military institution for the revolution without conspiring against it was a dilemma facing the Iranian revolution.

As mentioned, during the first year after the revolution, political authority was in the hands of the transitional government, led by Mehdi Bazargan. The left faction involved in the revolution, i.e., the People's Mojahedin Organization of Iran and Khalq guerrilla, was present on the Iranian political scene, as was the revolutionary Islamic movement that dominated the early stage of the Iranian Republic in the revolutionary courts. The left factions demanded the dissolution of the Iranian army and the demobilization of all its officers and soldiers. In the left's view, the army had been built to conform with the structure of the Pahlavi regime. It could not be made to fit the Islamic revolution and the Iranian people.[15] The transitional government, as a civilian authority, rejected the left's demand, as it believed that the dissolution of the army would lead to chaos. Mahdi Bazargan believed that the charges the leftists made against the Shah's army applied to all agencies in the country, with their varying specialties.[16] The leftist groups had waged a war of militias against the Shah's army and considered the dissolution of the army to be an announcement of victory over it. Meanwhile, the transitional government, composed of National Front elements that had participated in some governments under the Shah, reflected the stance of the national technocrat class, which had performed a political role under the Shah and an opposition role inside the regime.

The political Islam movement represented by Khomeini and his disciples saw the necessity of maintaining the army as part of the Iranian national fabric, but with restructuring. Its leaders were sent through revolutionary courts that sentenced 438 soldiers to death in one month.[17] In 14,000,1985 were sentenced to death, the majority of which were soldiers from army commanders to low-level troops.[18] Others were forced to retire.[19] However, there were calls for Khomeini to keep the army due to the dangers facing Iran, such as unrest in minority areas that were calling for independence one month after the revolutionaries took power in February 1979.[20] While the Iranian army was retained by the Iranian political system during the early years, especially the period before the war with Iraq, by 1980 its numbers had dropped 60% compared to its status before the revolution. The army's budget decreased similarly. This approach, which prevailed among the Iranian political elite during the first year of the revolution, quickly changed because of the developments in the Iraq-Iran war, which still affects the nature of the relationship between the army and the Iranian political elite as represented by the Supreme Leadership and the institutions of governance that he designated.

b. Revolutionary Guard

The Revolutionary Guard was characterized by periodic and rapid development. After the rebels' success, it was necessary to form an armed force that would fill the security and military voids that could have resulted from the collapse of the Shah's military and security institutions, whose members fled because they feared revolutionary punishment. The National Guard was founded; then its name changed to "Army of the Islamic Revolution Guards." Khomeini reaffirmed that the army of guards would have to follow the command of the interim civilian government, to maintain security and thwart conspiracies by the country institutions and foreign embassies. In February 1979,[21] Ibrahim

Yazdi and Hassan Lahouti took over the task of forming this armed force by assembling combat factions from among the rebel youth, such as the faction of Jawad Mansouri and the faction of Muhammad Montazeri, among others.[22] Ali Dansh Monfard was appointed the first commander of the Revolutionary Guards and used the headquarters of the Savak Organization (Organization of Intelligence and Security under the Shah) as his domicile.

Despite the establishment of the Revolutionary Guard, three revolutionary military organizations have operated independently of the Revolutionary Guard, the Guards of Revolution headed by Abbas Zamani with the support of Ayatollah Mousavi Ardabili, the Guards of Universities led by Muhammad Montazeri and supported by Ayatollah Beheshti (most of them trained in Lebanon), and the Armed Forces of the Islamic Mujahideen Organization led by Mohammad Brojerdi with the support of Murtaza Motaheri.[23] Some clerics remained independent by possessing armed organizations that played roles separate from the authority of the interim government. However, Hashemi Rafsanjani quickly reconsidered this matter and called for the unification of these combat organizations. On April,7 1979, the revolutionary council issued a decision to merge these organizations into the Revolutionary Guard, appointing Javad Mansouri as its leader, and after Abbas Zamani, known as Abu Sharif. Then the Revolutionary Guard was separated from the interim government under the authority of the Revolutionary Council.[24] As a result, the twelfth group[25] prepared the constitution of the Revolutionary Guard, consisting of nine articles with nine items attached. The Revolutionary Council ratified it. Accordingly, the Revolutionary Guard Command was formed and officially announced its presence on April 1979,22.[26] The Iranian Revolutionary Guard achieved several revolutionary goals such as joining non-clerical Islamic revolutionary forces and played the role of the revolutionary armed force with high enthusiasm and sectarian commitment. It maintained the ability to communicate with Iranian society and played a direct political role – as well as educational, cultural, and service roles – in society.

The Role

The role is what the Iranian legislator stipulated in the Constitution regarding the tasks entrusted to both the army and the Revolutionary Guard in cases of war and peace, taking into account the statements of Khomeini. It occupies the status of political legislation. The Iranian Constitution, issued in 1979 and amended in 1989, states in its preamble (entitled "The Sectarian Army"): "The focus is on building and equipping the country's armed forces to make sectarianism and faith a basis for this purpose. Therefore, the structure of the Army of the Islamic Republic and the Revolutionary Guard is based on the objective mentioned before. These armed forces are not only responsible for protecting and guarding the borders but also [for] the divine mission of jihad for the sake of Allah and the struggle for the extension of the rule of the divine law in the world (and prepare for them the power and strength of the horses that terrorize the enemy of God and your enemy and others without them)."[27] Article 3, section 3 provides for "the comprehensive strengthening of the national defense structure to the fullest extent, through military training for all individuals, to maintain the independence and territorial integrity of the country and preserve its Islamic regime."[28] Article 147 states: "In peacetime, the government can benefit from the personnel of the army and its technical equipment in the work of relief, education and production, and the Jihad of the building, taking into account the balance of Islamic justice without affecting the military readiness of the army negatively."[29] Article 150 states: "The Islamic Revolutionary Guard Corps, established in the early days of the victory of this revolution, should be consistent and firm in order to carry out its role in guarding the revolution and its gains. The law defines the functions and scope of these forces' responsibilities compar[ed] to [the] functions and responsibilities of other armed forces with an emphasis on cooperation and coordination among them."[30] It is clear from the previous Constitutional articles that the Iranian legislator stated the sectarian role of the military, whether the army or the Revolutionary Guard because it carries the divine message, which is Jihad and the struggle to extend the rule of divine law. Meanwhile, Article 150 was devoted to the necessity of continuity and of keeping the Revolutionary Guard. It left the role and function of the Revolutionary Guard to be determined by the laws that the Constitution does not regulate. Above all, we can see that the Iranian legislator wanted to create a Constitutional text that protected the Revolutionary Guard, as an abnormal military institution, and that left the matter of the nature of its role up to the Guard's regulating law, which can be changed based on the course of political life in Iran without the need for Constitutional amendments.

Degree of compatibility between the military and the political authority

The political authority that deals with the military institution in Iran is limited to the institution of the Supreme Leader without the institution of the presidency. The President of the Republic is restricted to establishing direct relations with the organs and leaders of the military institution in only the narrowest ways. Therefore, he cannot affect the performance and role of the military institution. This study will examine the level of compatibility between the military institution in both the army and the Guard, as well as the institution of the Supreme Leader. The Presidential institution's position regarding its relationship with the military might be joined with that of civilians. It is not a political authority that assumes sovereignty over the military institution.

First: The social composition of military institution members:

Members can join the military as permanent professional personnel by enrolling in the Iranian military colleges of the army and the Guard. A review of the conditions of admission to these military educational institutions reveals the social composition of members of the military institution.

Military colleges of the army

1. **Imam Ali University:** A specialized university for graduating officers of the Iranian army ground forces based in Tehran, founded during the era of Reza Shah in 1921 in the style of French military schools. In 1988, five colleges and a department of foreign languages were established inside the university. In 1996, its name changed from Officers' University to Imam Ali University of Officers.

2. **Imam Khomeini University:** A specialized university for graduating Iranian army naval officers, established in 1981 and based in the city of Nozhehr, Mazandaran province, north of Iran. It has six specialized colleges: Surface, Marine, Electronic Engineering and Maritime Communications, Mechanical Engineering, Maritime Administration, and Basic Sciences.[31]

3. **Shahid Stari University:** A specialized university for graduating officers in the Iranian Air Force, based in Tehran. It has six colleges: Aviation College, College of Air Engineering, College of Electrical Engineering, College of Computer Science, College of Management, and the Aviation College for Drones. It was launched in 2017.[32]

Military Colleges of the Revolutionary Guard

Imam Hussein University: A specialized university for graduating officers for the Revolutionary Guard. It was established by guide Ali Khamenei and includes five colleges: Security College, College of Intelligence, Faculty of Technology, College of Islamic Humanities, and College of Basic Jihadi Sciences. All Revolutionary Guard officers should graduate from Imam Hussein University, also known as the Revolutionary Guard Education University. After each faction of the Revolutionary Guard Corps members is recruited independently from the General Directorate of the Revolutionary Guard, all factions, including the representative of the Supreme Leadership of the Guard, the Basij forces, the intelligence department of the Guard, and the Quds Force, are obliged to graduate from Imam Hussein University.[33] Iran applies general conditions for enrolling in the military colleges, including physical and ideological conditions:

» To be Muslim.
» To believe in the Islamic Revolution and the Islamic Republic regime.
» To believe in and maintain a practical commitment to the Supreme Leadership.
» To not follow or support a party or political party.
» Priority shall be given to active members of the Basij forces and the sons of martyrs and war casualties.

The previous items were general conditions for admission to any Iranian military college which focuses on Islam for its applicants. This eliminates religious minorities such as Christians, Jews, and Zoroastrians, who, according to official statistics, formed 3% of the population of Iran in 2011.[34] Needless to say, this is a practice of discrimination. However, no article in the Iranian Constitution provides for full equality among the people, though some articles (14,13) recognize Christianity, Zoroastrianism, and Judaism as religious minorities that have the right to practice their religion freely under the law. Muslims must treat non-Muslims morally and with a sense of Islamic justice and equality, but the Constitution does not provide for full equality among the people. Iran does not have Shiism-specific military colleges, whether for the army or the Revolutionary Guard, but the general conditions for admission – such as belief in and practical commitment to the Supreme Leadership – exclude all Sunnis in Iran from entering military colleges. We are forced to rely on indications that Sunnis in Iran are not allowed to join the Iranian military institution due to the hardship involved in conducting an accurate census of Sunni officers in the Iranian military institution. However, a Sunni official has not assumed leadership of the Iranian military for the past forty years – the age of the Iranian Republic. One of the topics dealt with by the Iranian press was a Kurdi officer who ranked as military Brigadier, but the officer's biography indicated that he had joined the army before the revolution. During forty years of service, which included participation on the front line of the war with Iraq, he received only the rank of Brigadier.[35] No formal requirements prevent the entry of any Iranian into the military institution; candidates must simply maintain a sectarian and practical commitment to the Supreme Leadership and avoid joining or showing an inclination toward any political party or political organization (with the exception of some unwritten restrictions applied to the enrollment of Sunnis in the military institution). However, there is another type of discrimination with respect to enrollment: Priority is given to those who have memorized the Quran, those who are in Basij units, and those who are children of martyrs and war causalities. These individuals are few in number compared to all applicants. For example, 40,000 young Iranians applied to join the University of Imam Ali, and only 2,000 were accepted. This means that those with special priorities are almost always accepted. Considering all of the above, the Iranian military institution is open to the majority Shiite community in Iran, taking into account the lower sectarian conditions of joining than those of revolutionary guards. Thus, the Iranian military is not separate from the rest of society. The Iranian military institution cooperates with and confirms to the Supreme Leader institution in terms of its social structure. It is compatible with the social structure that supports the Supreme Leadership as head of the political authority dealing with the military institution and as the spiritual leader of the Iranian Shiite community that forms the military institutions' personnel.

Second: Making the political decisions of the military institution:

The political authority issues decisions that control the military institution and determine its military, societal, and sometimes political roles. The evaluation of these decisions determines the nature of the relationship between the political authority and the military institution, as well as the interaction of the military institution with civilians.

The political decisions of the military institution include:

- » The appointment of leaders.
- » The budgeting of the armed forces.
- » The military institution's political roles and its economic activities.

A- Appointment of the military institution's leader in Iran

According to the rules of the military leadership's hierarchy, the right of appointment derives from the right of loyalty. However, in the Iranian case, the Supreme Leader retains the right to appoint all military and security leaders in Iran. He appoints and dismisses:

- » The Chief of Joint Command.
- » The Commander-in-Chief of the Iranian Revolutionary Guard.
- » Senior leaders of the armed forces and internal security forces.

In 1989, the Iranian regime modified the hierarchy of leadership in the military, after realizing that the state of separation between multiple combat institutions led to reduced combat effectiveness during times of war. It also prevented coordination between them. As a result, the General Command of the Iranian armed forces – the highest military institution in Iran – was established to coordinate all Iranian armed forces and to manage the war during times of crisis through the strategic base Khatam Anbiya. This military commission is under the leadership of the Supreme Leader in accordance with Article 110 of the Constitution. It was formed at the end of the Iran-Iraq War due to differences between the Joint Command of the Army and the Revolutionary Guard. Initially, the Prime Minister was the General Command of the Armed Forces.[36] When Ali Khamenei became the Supreme Leader, he appointed Hassan Fayrouz Abadi as the General Command of the Armed Forces, a position he held from 1989 to 2016. He was replaced by Major General Mohammad Hussein Baqeri. The General Command of the Armed Forces leads forces in wartime and heads the general staff headquarters of the army, the Iranian Revolutionary Guard Corps headquarters, the headquarters of the police forces, and the Ministry of Defense and its constituencies. Its role in peacetime is centered on monitoring the branches of the military and security institution. In the hierarchy of Iranian military leadership, the Ministry of Defense and Logistics comes after the General Command of the Armed Forces. It performs the role of logistics and military manufacturing; its authority does not extend to military operations or the leadership of the armed forces. It is the only military commission whose president is appointed by the President of the Republic. The Ministry of Defense carries out all the administrative, financial, military, manufacturing, and training duties affecting the other military institutions, such as:

» Studying, developing, and collecting the military budget and distributing funds to all military bodies in coordination with the General Command of the Armed Forces.
» Managing military procurement internally and externally for both weapons and missions.
» Managing military property and defending the military institution's members before the judiciary.[37]

Despite the role of the General Command of the Armed Forces, which controls the rest of the forces, the Iranian regime was cautious to set the military leadership with parallel authority and leadership. There is not only a general military commander of the Iranian armed forces who comes under the Supreme Leader, the commander-in-chief of the armed forces but also a group of military leaders with separate duties and responsibilities. The General Command of the Armed Forces does not perform the direct role of commanding the forces and cannot move troops in peacetime. It can do so only by direct orders from the guide. This ensures that military power is not concentrated in one hand and that the military's loyalty to political power is guaranteed.

B- Budgeting of the armed forces

Iran's budget is within the average or below the average for military institution worldwide, compared to the gross domestic product; it reached 3.3% of the Iranian gross domestic product in 2016.[38] In fact, the Iranian public budget does not include all the revenues and expenses because of the parallel economy run by the Supreme Leader and its member from Awqaf, the companies owned by the Revolutionary Guard, and the funds of Hawza. However, the budget for the military institution has been a topic of debate, especially during the reign of President Hassan Rouhani. Although the governing party, with its president, has no control over the military institution, it still plans the development plan and the annual budgets of the country. The Iranian Republic has maintained a quinquennial development plan since its beginning in 1989. The negative impact of the war with Iraq during the first eight years left the country without a development plan because the country's potential had been directed toward the war effort. The first development plan (1994-1989) focused on the military institution, including rebuilding and equipping the defense infrastructure and providing needs according to specific defense objectives. The second development plan (1999-1994) aimed to decrease the funds of the regular armed forces and increase those of the revolutionary institutions, led by the Revolutionary Guard. The tenth item of this plan emphasized "strengthening and giving priority to the revolutionary forces by providing financial resources, government capabilities and giving priority to those who strive to consolidate the revolution and its values such as the fighter, activists, and Basijis."[39] Iranian President Hassan Rouhani tried to reduce the budget allocated to the Revolutionary Guard for the army during his first term (2017-2013). He presented a budget for 2017-2016 that reduced the Guard's budget, but his effort was in vain despite the fact that most parliamentarians had aligned with him.

Commission	Budget 2017-2018 (billion dol-lars)
Revolutionary Guards	7.9
Basij	0.4
Army	2.8
Ministry of Defense	1.2
Joint Leadership	0.9
Total Military Budget	13.5[40]

Rouhani aimed to reduce the influence of the Iranian Revolution Guard Corps, so that they would not pose a threat to the political life as they did with the former Iranian President Mohammad Khatami, but to a lesser extent with Rouhani, when a dispute broke out between Khatami and Khamenei over nuclear agreements in the oil sector. Rouhani's failure inside the parliament to amend the military budget proved that his impracticable authority over the military institution's budget, supposedly granted to him by the law through the Ministry of Defense, could be disabled by the authority of the Supreme Leader, aided by deputies in favor of him within the parliament. This could explain the separation of the budget from the authority of the Republic's president. At the same time, the Supreme Leader controls the budget of the military institution through huge financial resources outside the framework of the country's general budget. In addition, he maintains the ability to control the development or ratification of the budget within the parliament or through the Guardian Council and the Expediency Discernment Council if necessary.

C- The political and economic roles of the military institution

This axis is the major concern of the studies that deal with the nature of the relationship between the military institutions and the political authority because it evaluates this relationship. It also represents the interaction on both sides and its direct impact on civilians as the third party of the relationship.

The political practices of the Iranian military institution went through six stages:

1. **The stage of establishment and revolutionary work**: This extended from the announcement of the Revolutionary Guard's establishment to the outbreak of the Iraq-Iran war on September 1980,22. This period is characterized by the cleaning up of political disputes with the former regime. Similarly, the Revolutionary Guard surpassed the movement, seeking to overthrow the Republic regime. Examples include an attack from Noga Air Base, a coup attempt made by Sadiq Qutbzadeh (Minister of Foreign Affairs of the transitional government), the assassination of the Tudh Party and the Furqan group members, and the suppression of the separatist movements that broke out after the establishment of the Republic, especially after the referendum on the Constitution, which dissipated the rights of minorities and imposed the theory of Supreme Leadership. These separatist movements included those in Kurdistan and Western Azerbaijan and Ahwaz. In addition, the Revolutionary Guard served as a repressive force under the guise of protecting the revolution from its enemies.[41] The Revolutionary Guard suppressed Iran's cultural life by controlling the Supreme Council for Cultural Revolution, and by establishing laws that closed universities and eliminated administrative professors. It also allowed

cultural and media censorship, and thus played a major role in shaping the political thought of this stage as a dominant culture formed on the basis of loyalty to the revolution. According to the constitution of the Revolutionary Guard, which was ratified by the Revolutionary Council, the duty of the Revolutionary Guard is to confront elements and currents seeking to overthrow the Islamic Republic, whether by law or through the use of force.[42]

2. **The stage of transition to a semi-regular military force:** This was the stage of the Iraq-Iran war, during which the Revolutionary Guard became a semi-professional military force. It formed its combat, ground, air, and sea forces after its participation in the fight alongside the regular army, overthrowing Iranian President Ben Sadr, who rejected the method of people war. After Khomeini took over the war directly, the role of the Revolutionary Guard became that of a combat force.[43] Its involvement in the war reduced its political and security practices, but in return increased the rate of its acceptance among civilians. It competed with the Iranian regular army in combat skills, and it instilled revolutionary values, offering moral and sectarian guidance in army units.

3. **The stage of civil activities:** This period extended from the end of the Iran-Iraq war in 1988 to the beginning of President Mohammad Khatam's era in 1997. At this stage, despite the end of the Revolutionary Guard's combat missions during the war with Iraq, the political and religious status of the late Iranian President Hashemi Rafsanjani was not enough to stop the Iranian Revolution Guard Corps from interfering in political affairs. Strong relations linked Rafsanjani and Mohsen Rezai, commander of the Revolutionary Guard, throughout this stage. Rafsanjani had succeeded in his reconstruction and building plan, benefitting from Revolutionary Guard capabilities in the implementation of urban projects and infrastructure, especially the construction of dams and roads. This turned a large sector of the military institution, especially the Revolutionary Guard, into units for the implementation of urban projects.[44] Rafsanjani took advantage of military capabilities for his development project, distracting the military from interference in political affairs. This certainly enabled the Revolutionary Guard to assume power over economic institutions that increased the independence of the military in the face of political power.

4. **The stage of censorship and pressure on the authority of the President of the Republic:** The two periods of the presidency of the

former Iranian President Mohammad Khatami saw the rise of divergent reformist currents in their political alignments and their positioning on the regime. Along with the breakthrough in public freedoms and the extension of civil society institutions under Khatami the limit of criticism against the regime and the Supreme Leader personally was raised. As a result, the Revolutionary Guard commanders began to practice censorship over the authority of the president and threatened him with revolutionary forces to protect the revolution and its values as required by the Constitution and the law.[45] The Revolutionary Guard became involved in several political and security crises that broke out during Khatami's era, such as the events at Tehran University, the series of assassinations and physical assaults on symbols of the reformists (such as Said Hajarian and others), and press law crisis that led to a sit-in of parliamentarians.

5. **The stage of empowerment and the practices of sovereignty and economic hegemony:** This stage related to the presidency of Ahmadinejad (2013-2005), who was pushed into authority to remove the reform project and the political, intellectual, and cultural movement that was formed during the era of Mohammad Khatami. The Revolutionary Guard presence was prominent in Ahmadinejad's government. Accordingly, the Revolutionary Guard seized the administrative aspects of the state – in what was known as the administrative revolution during the Ahmadinejad era – by appointing conservatives, deputy ministers, and the general director of the retired Revolutionary Guard commanders. The Revolutionary Guard no longer maintained a parallel role in the country by dominating the Iranian government and the revolution. It regained its role in suppressing intellectuals, practicing censorship of newspapers, publications, and movies, and controlling Iranian embassies abroad.[46] The Guard also took over management of the automotive industry, and of cement and steel companies. At this stage, the Revolutionary Guard began carrying out illegal economic activities such as commodity smuggling through its platforms on the shores of the Arabian Gulf. Explicitly, the Iranian coastline on the Arabian Gulf and Iranian territorial waters were spheres of influence for the Revolutionary Guard and its navy. The Revolutionary Guard has also been carrying out money-laundering activities to fund its allied militias, such as Hezbollah, militias operating inside Syrian territory, and Iraqi Yemeni militias. This may refer to the economy of the proxy militias of the Guard outside Iranian territory. The Guard was also known to engage in drug trafficking; it cooperated

in this field with the Lebanese Hezbollah, and some of its leaders were arrested for their involvement in these crimes at the international level.[47]

6. **The stage of maintaining economic hegemony:** Economic conflict broke out between the institution of the presidency and the military institution with the signing of the nuclear agreement during the era of President Hassan Rouhani. The agreement opened, for Iran, the horizon of the world economy and the entry of foreign investment, especially in the Iranian oil sector. This started a clash between the Revolutionary Guard and Rouhani over the contracts for new oil investments, especially after Iranian Oil Minister Bijan Zanganeh stated his intention to sign oil contracts that focused on granting concessions to foreign companies – a move opposed by the Supreme Leader and the Revolutionary Guard.[48] After that, Rouhani acquiesced to the establishment of oil alliances between the Guard companies and some foreign companies, as happened in the investment contract of South Pars field.[49] However, these agreements did not stop the Guard from attacking and threatening Rouhani. This prompted the late Hashemi Rafsanjani to reform the cracked relationship between Rouhani on the one hand and the Supreme Leader and the Revolutionary Guard on the other hand. Still, their differences increased even more after Rafsanjani's death, as Rouhani criticized the Revolutionary Guard's dominance of the Iranian economy: "Part of the economy of the government which is without a gun has been changed to a state carrying a gun."[50] He meant that the Revolutionary Guard had the economy and weapons, while his demilitarized government had been deprived of economic activities and was then ordered to find a solution to people's economic problems. Rouhani faced another wave of confrontation with the Revolutionary Guard when he refused to open bank accounts for Revolutionary Guard entities in Iranian banks due to violations of the terms of an agreement that Iran signed under Ahmadinejad. Thus, Iran was placed atop a list of countries that practice money laundering. This prevented Iran from engaging in international banking transactions according to the terms of the nuclear agreement.[51] Accordingly, we can see that the political and economic role of the Revolutionary Guard increased even in peacetime and that it was associated largely with Supreme Leader Ali Khamenei. Therefore, the political affiliation of the Republic's president, whether reformist or conservative, was not considered due to the political interference of the Guard, despite Khatami's opposition to it. He was desperate to halt the Revolutionary Guard's ascendance

over elected political power in Iran. During the Ahmadinejad era, the political and economic influence of the Revolutionary Guard rose more quickly than it did during the Khatami era. During Ahmadinejad's first term (2009-2005), another political conflict arose between him (backed by the Guard and the Supreme Leader) and traditional conservatives headed by the late Hashemi Rafsanjani, who supported the reformers to a certain extent or at least followed the traditional methods in their political rivalry with the reformists. The Revolutionary guard won the Iranians' favor at certain periods, such as during the war with Iraq and the reconstruction period. However, the Guard's repressive practices against Iranian intellectuals and artists created a bad image of the military institution in the civilian mind, as did the Revolutionary Guard's dominance of economic activities. The latter disturbed both ordinary citizens and businessmen who were no longer able to compete with Revolutionary Guard companies because of the government concession granted to the Guard's subsidiaries.

Third: Methods of Recruitment

Iran was the first country in the Middle East to apply conscription laws. The first law dealing with compulsory recruitment in Iran dated back to 1924, with the beginning of the National State Project. Compulsory recruitment is the pillar upon which the Iranian national sentiment was created, as the other elements are vulnerable in Iran, especially in terms of Iranian homogeneity. The Iranian Constitution provides for the compulsory recruitment of all Iranian males (except in cases excluded by law).[52] Article 4 of the Military Service law, ratified in 1984, stipulates that the duration of compulsory conscription in Iran is thirty years and is divided into four stages: the compulsory service (two years), the reserve (eight years), the first phase of military support (ten years), and the second phase of military support (ten years).[53]

» The current period of compulsory recruitment has been reduced to twenty-one months, twenty months of service in remote areas, nineteen months in border areas, with further reductions in the duration of conscription based on academic qualification. The duration of service for someone with a bachelor's degree was reduced by one month, with a master's degree by two months, and with a Ph.D. by three months. In 2011, however, these reductions were abolished and the service period was twenty-one months for everyone. In 2012, the third son became exempt from recruitment, though this, too, was canceled. Likewise, a cash allowance can obtain exemption from compulsory recruitment; this was implemented for the first time in 2008. Someone who is absent from duty will pay $500. (3600 tomans per dollar).[54] In 2016, the Rouhani government introduced a proposal to determine a five-year absence period to replace the compulsory recruitment with a cash allowance. However, the General Staff of the Iranian armed forces rejected the proposal. Then the Iranian parliament set it at eight years.

The cash allowance ranged from $2,700 to $13,900.[55] The law determined the amount of the fines or the so-called purchase period of conscription service according to the applicant's educational degree as follows:

- » Below secondary school, 100 million riyals, equivalent to $2,222 (45,000 riyals per dollar).
- » High school (diploma), 150 million riyals ($3,333).
- » Intermediate institute, 200 million riyals ($4,444).
- » Bachelor's degree, 250 million riyals ($5,555).
- » PhD, 300 million riyals ($6,666).
- » Ph.D. in medicine, 350 million riyals ($7,777).
- » Specialized doctors and consultants, 500 million riyals ($11,111).[56]

The impact of compulsory recruitment on the military's relationship with civilians

Supposedly, conscription reduces the compatibility of the military and the political authority. Because most members of the military are civilians for a period of time, and then return to their civilian life after their service. Compulsory recruitment creates a sense of solidarity between civilians and the military institution, as the military institution harmonizes its civilian members with general rules of engagement in the military institution, whether at the level of officers or individuals. In the Iranian case, we can detect a selective discrimination regarding who is fit for either the army's or the Revolutionary Guard's recruiting bodies, which is the favorite option for young members because of the advantages they receive during service and even after it. Commitment is assessed by the Basij units and their departments in schools and neighborhoods. Undoubtedly, ethnic, religious, and linguistic minorities find it difficult to join the Guard. This affects the rule of equality in recruitment among citizens.

The trend toward rejecting compulsory recruitment inside Iranian society

Recently, there has been a wave of rejection of the practice of conscription in Iran, with calls for it to become a voluntary system. The reasons for this include:

» **An increase in the number of deserters:** Official statistics place the number of deserters from military service in Iran at 1.5 million.[57] They flee from service for several reasons. Key among these reasons are economic conditions. With low incomes and high dependency among Iranian families, especially in tribal and rural communities, Iranian citizens cannot readily participate in compulsory service because they have no money to cover their expenses and those of their families. Military recruits receive low salaries. For instance, a recruit receives 34.250 tomans ($7.50) per month. Essentially, military service, for recruits, is like unpaid labor. Due to the horrific financial situation that Iranian soldiers face, the Iranian parliament passed a law in 2017 obliging the government to pay at least 150,000 toman ($33) a month. In addition, a law in Iran obliges the government to pay 60% to 90% of the public servant salary for the recruit during his conscription.[58]

» **A lack of professionalism and low quality of training among Iranian soldiers:** During the past three years, several Iranian soldiers have died because of their colleagues' misuse of weapons, or due to non-compliance with security and safety rules inside camps and barracks. The most prominent of these incidents occurred in August 2017, when a recruit fired on his colleagues during training, killing four and injuring dozens. Incidents like this occur on a monthly basis.

» **The prevalence of suicide among recruits:** Suicide is remarkably common among recruits, according to statements from Iranians who were colleagues of soldiers who committed suicide. The reasons for these suicides range from insults received from higher ranking soldiers during military service to ridicule because of one's ethnicity or religious background. In some cases, recruits commit suicide because they are addicted to drugs and cannot cope with the sudden abstinence required in military service. Also, a lack of leave (and the short duration of leave) as well as service far from a recruit's home have led to suicides.[59] The draft law on conscription was intended to support a degree of compatibility between the military and civilians, but the enactment of military service cash laws accompanied with low salaries for soldiers and psychological and physical pressures placed on Iranian recruits led to a deep hatred of the Iranian military institution among young Iranians. The connection between the Revolutionary Guard and the institution of the Supreme Leader also led to these negative feelings, as did civilians' resentment of political power. Thus, the status of recruitment and its laws is a factor limiting the compatibility of the military and most civilians, as well as members of the elected political authority. However, these factors do not negatively affect the relationship between the political authority and the institution of the Supreme Leader because the Supreme Leader seeks to obtain the largest number of soldiers at the lowest financial cost while ignoring all elements of social peace and security as well as public satisfaction. The institution seeks to please the high ranks of the military and grants them financial concessions for putting pressure on recruits.

Results and future outlook

A study of the analysis levels of the relationship between the Iranian military institution and the political authority institution shows the following:

» Political authority in Iran is divided into two distinct institutions: the institution of the Supreme Leader and the institution of the presidency. The first one is effective at dealing with the military institution, and the second one is largely marginalized and unable to deal with the military institution, nor with the military's dominating role over the presidency. The role of the elected political authority in relation to the military is limited to providing support services for military industries and directing budget allocations to the military institution through the Ministry of Defense, which has limited powers in military action.

» The Iranian military is divided into two main factions. The first is the regular army, and the second is the Revolutionary Guard, which competes with the regular army in terms of its responsibilities to defend Iranian territory against external aggression. The army does not compete with the Revolutionary Guard in terms of defending the values of the revolution and the political, cultural and societal roles it has.

» As a result of the formation, condition, and the role that the army and the Revolutionary Guard played in the revolution at the beginning of the presidency, political power (i.e., the institution of the Supreme Leader) shows a great deal of bias in favor of the Revolutionary Guard.

» The social composition of the military supports compatibility between the military institution and the political authority. There are no biases with respect to the selection of officers in the military, and there is no closed society among the Iranian military elite (with the exception of religious minorities, who are barred from enrolment in elite military institutions). This approach is less applicable if ethnic minority elements are admitted to revolutionary institutions at an early stage. The second exception of the social composition harmony concept for the military institution with the political authority, especially the practical commitment to the principle of the Supreme Leader, which leads to a sort of societal classification on the basis of sects and opens the door to selection processes that proceed according to an unspecified standard facilitating mediation and nepotism. Nevertheless, the Iranian military is not considered a closed society on a certain level within Iranian society.

» The mechanisms of political decision-making within the military at the level of the appointment of military leaders reflects the hegemony of the Supreme Leadership over the military and creates a kind of parallel authority between the base and the military. Therefore, the tasks of commanding forces were distributed among a number of leaders, despite the formation of a coordinating commission that exists between the forces. Its president is the highest military authority in the regime, but his authority is limited to circumstances of war. In the case of peace, each military institution is managed separately and by direct reference to the Supreme Leader personally.

» The Supreme Leader restricts the elected government's authority in terms of budgeting the military through his control of a group in the Iranian parliament. He retains for himself financial resources that are not included in the public budget, and he manages a parallel economy in the country. This gives him an advantage over the military. For this reason, the elected political authority cannot manage the military's budget.

» The institution of the Supreme Leader guides the political practices of the military institution. In most cases, these are directed against the elected political authority. Therefore, this does not represent a traditional conflict within the government between the political authority and the military, as it is a mechanism of the country's administration and the regime system of the Supreme Leader.

» The Revolutionary Guard's economic activities have been aggravated to such an extent that both the governmental sector's and the private sector's growth have been hindered and have become the focus of conflict between the President and the Supreme Leader in the administration of current President Hassan Rouhani.

» The system of recruitment in the Iranian military is the biggest weakness in the standards of compatibility between the military, the political authority, and civilians. At the public level, the military's image collapses because of the cash allowance, discrimination, and low salaries. This increases desertions from duty, as well as suicides and the killing of comrades. It also increases the gap between the political authority (i.e., the institution of the Supreme Leader) and civilians. The lower and middle ranks within the military resent the institution of the guide. The goal of military service becomes seeking promotion to give one the ability to seize funds via the economic institutions of the Revolutionary Guard or by practicing illegal economic activities covered by the military rank.

» The Supreme Leader's dominance of the military stems from Ali Khamenei's existence as Supreme Leader. During this time, the Iranian military is subordinated to Ali Khamenei more than to the institution of the Supreme Leader. Remarkably, the military's loyalty cannot move smoothly to a new Supreme Leader After Khomeini's death. As known, IRGC participates in the selection of a new Supreme Leader, or it overthrows the clerical institution; then a military dictatorship replaces the rule of clerics, especially with Khamenei's insistence on not appointing a deputy until now.

» Real reforms cannot easily be carried out at the level of the political system or progress in public freedoms because of the Supreme Leader and the military institution. Consequently, a state of public tension and total rejection of the regime will become more pronounced, especially among the young Iranians, as well as among those economically affected by the Iranian Revolutionary Guard Corps' economic dominance over the Iranian economy.

Endnotes

(1) Ibrahim, Shadia Fathi. «Civil Military Relations and Democratic Transition: An Analytical Study of Theoretical Trends.» Al Nahda Magazine, October 10,2006.

(2) Abdullah, Masri. «How to Reduce the Role of the Army in Political Life?» Almanasah. March 2017. http://cutt.us/UiVv8.

(3) Abdullah, Masri. "Why Democracy in the Arab Region Fails?" al Mohtwa. http://cutt. us/JGrO.

(4) Hamada Mohammad Attia, Abdel Rahman. The Military Institution and Opportunities for Democratic Transformation. Arab Democratic Center. http://cutt.us/wtE47.

(5) Mostafa, Kavakbian. "The Conceptualism of Religious Democracy, Others." http://cutt. us/PsyWa.

(6) Islamic Republic of Iran. Association of Culture and Islamic Relations - Directorate of Translation and Publication. Constitution of the Islamic Republic in Iran. 16 .1997.

(7) The Supreme Leader institution means the person of the Supreme Leader and his office, the House of Supreme Leader, including his consultants and representatives, who are deployed in all organs of the state without exception, as well as the institutions of governance that he forms or in which he participates, such as the Guardian Council and the Expediency Council.

(8) Council of Experts: A council whose members are exclusively religious jurists. Its mission is to choose a Supreme Leader. Its term of membership

is eight years. Its members are elected by free elections from the people. The Iranian Constitution, Article 107.

(9) The Guardian Council is composed of twelve jurists, six of whom are appointed and six of whom are ratified, after the nomination of the president of the judiciary and the president of the parliament. It supervises all electoral processes and validates the eligibility of candidates to run for a term of six years. The Iranian Constitution, Articles 98,94, and 99.

(10) "%63 Increase in IRGC Contribution from Budget 96." Radio Zamaneh. http://cutt. us/WCjCz.

(11) Hassan, Haifa Rashid. "The Political Role of the Military Institution. The Israeli Military Institution as a Model." Journal of Law for Legal and Political Sciences: 418.

(12) Osama, Al-Ghazali Harb. Revolutionary War… Its Concept and Contemporary Developments. Master's thesis, Cairo University, 17 .1978.

(13) Hassan, Hamdi Abdel Rahman. Military and Governance in Africa with Application to Nigeria. Master's thesis, Cairo University, 16 .1985.

(14) Imam and the Army (from 1964 to 1980) Codification of Ideological and Political Administration of the Iranian Army. January 1982.

(15) Salhi, Suhrab. A Study on Contemporary Iranian Developments. Tehran: Imam Hussein University Publications, 2008.

(16) Ali Bazargan, Abd. Problems and Issues of the First Year of the Revolution. Tehran: Dar Nahdat Azadi, 33 .1984.

(17) "Those Who Were Destitute After the 1979 Revolution: From Amir Abbas Hoyda to Berri Blanda." Deutsche Welle. http://cutt.us/srm7r.

(18) Fathi, Ihsan. "Statistics and Figures of Executions Between 1979 and 61) 2017 Thousand Executions)." Al-Arabiya. http://cutt.us/Oieu4.

(19) Donald, Zaccherl. "The Influence of the Islamic Revolution on the Iranian Army." Najin Iran Magazine (Iran's Emerald), Summer 115,2011.

(20) Kenneth, Katzman. The Revolutionary Guards, Its Origins and Composition. Emirates Center for Studies and Research. 8.

(21) "The History of the Founders and Founders of the Revolutionary Guards." Qatra. http://cutt.us/wkhzd.

(22) "Three Novels About the Establishment of the Revolutionary Guards." The ISNA Agency. http://cutt.us/YdDAd.

(23) "History of the Founders and Founders of the Revolutionary Guards." The Site of Andishe Ha. http://cutt.us/EKXcq.

(24) Revolution Council: Khomeini announced its establishment on January 1979,12, before the announcement of the revolution's success. However, the formation of the council began months earlier, according to a letter that Khomeini sent from his exile in Paris to Ayatollah Morteza Muttahari. The

letter asked Muttahari to assemble the revolutionary elements in a council so that they would not face trouble for not recognizing the revolutionary elements when they returned and overthrew the Shah, and to include the elements outside Iran. The council practiced its authority on the first day of Khomeini's arrival in Iran. He commissioned Mahdi Bazarajan to form the interim government. He ran Iran after the resignation of the government and also supervised the referendum on the regime and the administration until the election of the first Iranian government headed by Beni Sadr. Source: Imam Newspaper, p. 5, p. 426.

(25) The group of twelve was formed by Ibrahim Yazdi as the assistant head of the transitional government for the revolution upon the interim government's request to discuss the formation of an armed force to maintain internal security. Ibrahim Yazdi formed the group consisting of Hassan Lahouti, Mohsen Sajgara, Murtadhi Al-Waiari, Ali Mohammad Basharti, Mohammad Ghuti, Hassan Jafari, Ali Farzayn, Dharabi, Asgar Sabbaghian, Tehranzhi, and Ali Danesh Monfarid. The group held its first meetings in Baghah, during the first half of February 1979. Guards of the Islamic Revolution, "The Voice of Freedom."

(26) "The History of the Founders and Founders of the Revolutionary Guards." Qatra. http://cutt.us/wkhzd.

(27) Islamic Republic of Iran. Association of Culture and Islamic Relations - Directorate of Translation and Publication. Constitution of the Islamic Republic in Iran. 16 .1997.

(28) Ibid., 26.

(29) Ibid., 120.

(30) Ibid., 150.

(31) "The Cultural and Media Headquarters in the Naval Rorces of the Islamic Republic of Iran." Imam Khomeini University of Science and Marine Arts in the city of Nuhshehr. http://cutt.us/nw91K.

(32) Shaheed Stari University for Air Science. http://cutt.us/msJv3.

(33) University of Imam Hussein. http://www.ihu.ac.ir/.

(34) "A Look at the Numbers of Religious Minorities During the Past Half Century in Iran." The Iranian Statistics Center. http://cutt.us/76bQM.

(35) "Dialogue with a Sunni leader Received the Rank of Dean + Photos." Mashrigh Website. http://cutt.us/GqXtw.

(36) "The Status of the Armed Forces in the Islamic Republic of Iran." Hassoun Magazine, Spring 164,2008.

(37) "The Iranian Constitution Group, Which Includes: The Constitution with Its Amendments for 1990. Theories of the Council of Interpretation and Advisory of the Constitution, Tehran, 505 ".1991-1990.

(38) "How Much is the Middle East Defense Budget?" Akhbar News. http://cutt.us/xfzmj.

(39) Ali Dre, Nukarani. "An Overview of Policy-Making in the Defense Infrastructure of the Islamic Republic of Iran." Quarterly Political Policy Approach 2, no. 3 (Spring 193:(2012.

(40) "How Much Is the Budget of Military Institutions in Iran. Ali Qudai. http://cutt.us/ zaHl1.

(41) Mehdi, Nisr Bor. "The Role of the Revolutionary Guard in the Continuity of the Islamic Revolution." Husoun Magazine, Fall 2009. http://cutt.us/E160v.

(42) Mahmoud, Akbari, and Joach Haq Ju. "The Jurisprudential and Juristic Approach to the Entry of the Revolutionary Guard Into the Field of Culture in Order to Achieve the Message of Guard." Quarterly Studies of the Islamic Revolution 5, no. 86:(2017) 19.

(43) Ismail Mansouri, Larijani. History of Sacred Defense. Tehran: Dar Redha Publishing. 155-150,2004.

(44) "A Look at a Quarter of a Century of the Performance of the Revolutionary Guard." Cultural Assistant in the Revolutionary Guards, Tehran. 29 .2005.

(45) "The Full Text of the Message of the Leaders of the Revolutionary Guard to Khatami." Aftab News. http://cutt.us/xbSir.

(46) "Revolutionary Guard and Ahmadinejad Are Swallowing All the Companies and State Factories." Peck Iran. http://cutt.us/cbODK.

(47) Mahmoud, Bustani. "The Role of the Revolutionary Guard in the Drug Trade Around the World." Al Ahwaz Al Mazloma. http://cutt.us/EThtY.

(48) "New Rouhani›s Letter of the Guide on the New Oil Contracts, the Site of Online Economy." http://cutt.us/Ec9on.

(49) Iran and Total Sign the First New Oil Agreement to Develop Phase 11 of the Southern Faris Field." Sarbush Economy. http://cutt.us/t2vsg.

(50) "Why Did Rouhani Address the Revolutionary Guards by Saying 'A Government Carrying a Gun'?" Iran Website. http://cutt.us/PquNP.

(51) "FATF Compulsory Success for Rouhani to Restrict Revolutionary Guard. Financial Times. http://cutt.us/jiMxO.

(52) The Iranian Constitution, Article 151.

(53) "Will the Period of Military Service Be Reduced?" Site Sarat. http://cutt.us/HY15z. 54-The Fever of Purchasing Compulsory Military Service Exemption and the Reactions to This in the Regulations of 2017: Between Earning Returns and Class Gap." The Young

(54) Journalists Club Agency. http://cutt.us/2UnKq.

(55) The General Duty Service Law, ratified by the Parliament on October 1984,21, with amendments until August 2017,8. http://cutt.us/QcVUW.

(56) "The Amount of Soldiers› Salaries According to the Academic Certificate Between 2017 and 2018." The Voice of the Educational Counselor. http:// cutt.us/EUzSA.

(57) "The Number of Absentees Covered y the Resolution is 1 Million and 500 Persons /Fine Ranging from 20 to 50 Million Toman for the Absentees." The Young Journalists Club Agency. http://cutt.us/QhVyT.

(58) "The Council Approves the Minimum Wage of 150 Thousand Toman." Aftab. http:// cutt.us/fpCCe.

(59) Heidi, Fahimeh Khidr. "Military Service in Iran; The Process That Is Supposed to Make a Young Man. http://cutt.us/ZAjgu.

The Military Doctrine of the Iranian Armed Forces Considering the Dual Army and the Revolutionary Guards

Mo'taz Mohammad Salama (Ph.D.)
Director of the Arabian Gulf Program at Al-Ahram
Center for Political and Strategic Studies

Introduction

The issue of the Iranian military doctrine – with respect to the dual sides, i.e., the army and Revolutionary Guard – is of great importance. There is a great deal of ambiguity in this doctrine, which is anchored by the duality of the formation of the Iranian armed forces. The central pillar of the armed forces is represented by the Revolutionary Guard, while the army is secondary in importance. This dual status is intentionally guided by the Iranian regime, which uses it to instill specific convictions and principles regionally, unrelated to the essence of the military doctrine. In this case, the Iranian military doctrine seems to be torn between different tasks and objectives between the Guard and the army. This, in turn, creates a spiral of ambiguity and contradictions because the army is a non-politicized national institution that purportedly defends the nation against external threats. Unlike the Revolutionary Guard, the army is not a revolutionary institution, nor does it defend the Islamic regime that took power in 1979.[1]

Though it is smaller than the army, the Guard has become the primary military force for many reasons, including the very nature of the Revolutionary Guard, which came into existence as a shield and spearhead of the Iranian Republic and which formed the second security pillar of the Iranian regime, along with the intelligence and security apparatuses.[2] In addition to its unique composition, the Guard maintains the role of protecting the revolution from its enemies, as well as maintaining the revolution's ideological purity and its link to the regime's political future, doing so by protecting the revolution from enemies at home and abroad. With this extension of the Guard, the army's position in the regime shrank after the revolution because of its American background and its support of the opposition.[3]

The issue of Iranian military doctrine becomes more important as the Iranian military chooses to reinforce ideological and political trends. The previous conditions, created by the army itself, lacked a military doctrine concerning the country and instead centered its allegiance on the person; it served as the Shah's army and not as the army of the homeland, which made it a weak institution despite its historical existence.[4]

First: The Constitution, principles, and creating a military doctrine

The doctrine ingrained in the Iranian Constitution has overwhelmed the institutional and ideological framework governing the armed forces, their role and their status within the country. The Constitution has created a doctrinal country protected by its institutions, foremost among them the armed forces. The Constitution's preamble states: "The priority on building and equipping the country's armed forces is for making faith and doctrine a base for that." Also, it mentions that the armed forces are "not only ... responsible for protecting and guarding the border, but also the divine mission and the struggle to extend the rule of the divine law in the world." [5]

The Constitution makes clear that the regime's sectarianism and political objective dominates military doctrine. This is more prominent in the Revolutionary Guard than in the army. However, the Constitution places the protection of the revolutionary regime, including its sectarian and political vision, at the center of the armed forces doctrine. Furthermore, it emphasizes the people's responsibility to protect the regime. The Constitution highlights the dominance of the divine goal for the armed forces. Thus, the regime's fundamental aim was not to establish a professional military focusing on national security but to develop an army motivated by the religious and sectarian aims of carrying the burden of the divine message according to the teachings of the Twelver doctrine.

In the Constitution, section 3 of Chapter 9 provides detailed articles about the army that firmly establish a link between the military doctrine of the armed forces and the political doctrine of the country. Article 143 defines the army's role as defending the country's independence and territorial integrity as well as the regime of the Islamic Republic. The Constitution imposes on the army the country's Islamic character as approved by the regime of the revolution. Article 144 states that the army must be "an Islamic army that must be a doctrinal and populist army and it must include decent individuals who believe in the aims of the Islamic revolution, and even sacrificing themselves to achieve it." This does not require physical and psychological "fitness" on the part of the armed forces, but rather a mentality that believes in the aims of the Islamic revolution. This suggests that individuals who do not believe in the Islamic Republic's system are excluded from recruitment.

In addition to the articles on the army, two special constitutional articles focus on the Revolutionary Guard. These are articles 150 and 151. Article 150 stipulates that the Guard is to "firmly ... play its role in guarding the revolution and its gains." This means that the Guard is entrusted with the security of the revolutionary state and the Republic regime. It seems that those who drafted the Constitution were aware that a conflict over competence and duties was expected between the Guard and the army. The same article stipulates that "the law defines the limits of the duties of these forces (Guard) and the scope of their responsibility with regard to the duties and the scope of other armed forces while emphasizing the coordination among them." The Revolutionary Guard articles distinguish between the Guard's internal and external duties and defines them as follows: Protecting the revolution and its security, suppressing all forces opposing it, supporting liberation movements throughout the world, and guarding the leaders and their objectives from the American and Zionist enemy and their agents in the region. The Guard's duties include protecting scientists and borders to prevent weapons smuggling, as well as to detect spies and to patrol roads and cities to provide security and eliminate separatists.[6] The Constitution made the people a partner in the task of defending the country and the regime of the Islamic Republic. Similarly, Article 151 states that "the government is responsible for preparing the programs and the necessary means of military training for all people that confirm the Islamic standards so that all its members have the ability to defend the country and the Islamic Republic of Iran." Article 152 of the Constitution stipulates that the foreign policy of the Republic of Iran shall be based on the prohibition of any domination or submission and shall preserve the country's full independence and territorial integrity. Article 154 affirms that "the Islamic Republic of Iran supports the legitimate struggle of the vulnerable against the proud in any part of the world." Regarding the political and military doctrine, the Constitution contains a significant contradiction between internal principles and those practiced externally. While Article 152 of the Constitution states that the foreign policy of the Republic of Iran should not be based on any kind of domination and should maintain the country's full independence and territorial integrity, Article 154 affirms that "the Islamic Republic of Iran supports the legitimate struggle for the oppressed against the proud in any part of the world." In practical terms, the regime's multifaceted ideology has influenced the armed forces doctrine, as the regime sends to the outside world various facets of its identity, including the Islamic one, which strives to address all Muslims. Under this cover is the Shiite identity, which invisibly represents the Persian national identity. This multi-faceted approach presents Iran as a "message of destiny" to lead the Muslim world and become a regional "superpower" in the Gulf, the middle of the Arab world, and Central Asia.[7] Over several historical periods (the Persian Empire, the Islamic conquest, the Safavid dynasty, the Qajar dynasty, the Pahlavi in the 20th century, and the Islamic Revolution of 1979), Iran maintained a troubled relationship with modernity and its dual religious and political character. Many of these contradictions were transfe rred to the post-revolutionary era. These overlapping factors af f ected the structure of the Iranian armed forces and its divisi o n between the traditional professional army and the ideologica l ly driven Revolutionary Guard, as well as the military ideology that focuses on defensive and asymmetrical warfare against the United States.[8] In addition, Iran presents itself as a nation that inherited an ancient civilization, one providing cultural treasures to th e world from centuries before Islam. At the same time, Iran suffers from a sense of strategic deprivation, abuse, isolation, and historical injustice under which it experiences the mirage of conspiracy t heories, seeing itself as a stranded country facing threats from foreigners who plan to deprive it of its legitimate rights.[9] Accordingly, Iran has faced a difficult question: Is it a global Islam ic project or is it a Shiite sectarian project? At the official level exists a denial of any accusations that the Republican project is a s ectarian project. Some are tempted to portray Iran as an example of Islamic enlightenment in the world,[10] but its practices reveal an important role for sectarianism in Iranian policy, both interna l ly and externally.[11] Exporting the revolution, the doctrine of spreading jihad, and the strengthening of Persian influence under the guise of spreading Islam are the fundamentals of the political doctrine of the Iranian Republic and the IRG in particular. Iran considers its revolution to be representative of the Islamic world, Sunni, and Shiite. It did not restrict itself to the sectarian Shiite context by supporting Sunni and Shiite groups equally; it made defending Iran a religious obligation that would spread Iranian influence throughout the Muslim world. Clausewitz's statement has proven that religion is an extension of Iranian politics by other means. By "exporting" its model of Islam and its political system, Iran seeks to strengthen its hold in the Arab world and reintegrate it into the modern Iranian empire.[12] The doctrine of the Iranian Republic stems primarily from the military lessons it learned while seeking effective and practical solutions to the security challenges facing Iran within the framework of its ideological and geostrategic goals. The competition between the army and Revolutionary Guard structures will persist, though the Republic leadership is actively seeking to improve the viability of their joint efforts.[13] Decision- making efforts surrounding national security issues go back to the Supreme Leader with a narrow circle of revolutionary veterans. Their involvement in decision-making is based on their informal, rather than their official, status. A smaller group of senior military and security commanders protects national defense and security policy in Iran and serves as the commander's "information guards."[14]

To maximize the benefits of ideological indoctrination, the regime propagates the ideology among the people and the army, seeking to present the positive side of the regime's dominance. In addition, its existence in the army reduces differences among the various military structures. Along with this, the military cannot take power from civil institutions engaged in the regime's political program. Thus, the regime devotes itself to God and depicts its agenda as divine will.[15] The military doctrine dominates the country and the army, and is assisted by Iranian society, which is continuously mobilized to construct museums that commemorate martyrs and to create information banks and archives that preserve and reproduce military history, simulating the tragic recall of the martyrdom of Imam Hussein. The regime's exhibitions and museums focus on the Shah's prisons, the martyrs of the revolution, and the martyrs of the Iraq-Iran war. They include documentaries and video footage. In addition, commissions are given for the construction of statues that commemorate military memories and heroism, costing the regime millions of dollars annually. All these activities on the part of the regime spread the concept that the defense of the homeland is sacred and highlight the expansion of Iranian power as a result of the Iran-Iraq war.[16] The Revolutionary Guard controls the formation of military doctrine by monopolizing the official narrative of the Iraq-Iran war. Although governmental and non-governmental institutions in Iran have released leaflets about the war, the Guard is responsible for the biggest share of the military narrative. The Guard's studies cover a wide range of subjects and curricula, including proposals about the war in the Koran, a series of important battles, and a detailed and analytical chronology of the war.[17] Videos about the Iranian armed forces, as well as the regulations and curricula taught in Iran's military academies, indicate the dominance of Twelver Shiism. On various occasions, the Iranian army's displays have included shouts from soldiers devoted to Imam Ali and the Supreme Leader, confirming their belief in the absent Imam and Haidariyah sectarianism.[18] This sectarian trend is reflected in exercises, military songs, and orders.

This fact is reinforced by the spread of the Guard's and the Basij's doctrine and principles in the civil system, especially in the economy and in education. The educational system prioritizes ideology over everything, and the Basij is a tool for instilling the Guard's doctrine in the educational system and academic institutions. Therefore, the Basij established the lecturer Basij Organization (LBO), which comprises %25 of the total lecturers in Iran, and the student Basij Organization (SBO), which comprises 650,000 student members from 700 institutions in Iran.[19] In addition, Iran is raising children from the age of three years with revolutionary ideology and the principles of the revolution and the Basij. The military displays of the army and the Revolutionary Guard reveal that the supervision of battles and wars is conducted intricately, which is why it is called a "mosaic doctrine." However, it seems that their ability to deal with multiple variables and battlefields is akin to guerrilla warfare rather than reflecting a war strategy employed by an organized professional army. Although they may suffer defeat in a major battle, they can manage small battles, inflicting significant losses on their opponents. Thus, Iran has mastered asymmetrical warfare; it maintains a historical background in such warfare, as well as in low-intensity wars and proxy wars.[20] The principle of Iranian defense is based on deterring any expected attack against the Islamic Republic by sacrificing massive numbers. For instance, many Basij fighters act like civilians and allow invading forces to pass through them, then attack the forces – a style akin to what one sees in gang wars.[21]

Second: The Pasdaranisation of the community and the country's ideology

Since the revolution in 1979 and the establishment of the Revolutionary Guard during the same year, the Guard has assumed a unique position at the center of the revolutionary system and within the Iranian community, as well as with the Supreme Leader of the Republic. The Guard is the institution of the Supreme Leader, to whom it owes allegiance, and enjoys several privileges, such as relative independence from the Supreme Leader himself. While the Guard intervenes in the affairs of other institutions, agencies, and ministries, it remains the most independent institution in terms of managing its own affairs without interference from other institutions.[22] The Guards has set up its own theological institutes, such as Shahid Mahawali University, which politically and ideologically mobilized officers and recruits. The army infiltrated clergy members who were political and ideological; some of them were graduates of Shahid Mahawali University.[23]

The Guard gained this particular position by recruiting members and ideologically dominating their identity as well as their professional lives. The members become a "delegate" of the Guard wherever they are, carrying with them extremism covered by religious sanctity and using revolutionary slogans.[24] The members of the Guard are known for their religious enthusiasm, their absolute loyalty to the regime, and their readiness to defend the regime against "domestic and foreign enemies." This has given them an honored status among the leadership as well as a significant influence within the state apparatus at the political and economic levels.

During the period between 1979 and 1982, when the Islamic Republic was struggling for survival, the Revolutionary Guard proved itself to be the regime's ultimate weapon after it suppressed the uprisings of the Kurdish, Baloch, and Turkmen separatists, and after striking the "People's Mujahideen" after its public clash with Khomeini in June 1981, which posed the most serious threat to the Islamic Republic.[25] At first, the Guard was not a dominant military force; many of its initial activities focused on guarding important individuals in the new regime and maintaining public order. However, its size, power, and influence increased steadily as the regime sought to strengthen its authority.[26]

The Guard is assisted by a massive number of volunteers from the Basij, whose followers consist of recruits and young volunteers, most of them between the ages of 11 and 17, who come from rural areas or poor districts and who have limited education.[27] Saeed Gul-Kar explains how the Basij became a parallel society inhibiting the existence of civil society. It even became part of official state apparatuses through its presence in schools and universities, as well as among the workforce, including lawyers, doctors, and other sectors of society.[28] The Basij cooperates with law enforcement forces to ensure security in large urban centers.[29]

"Pasdaranisation" may be the best term for describing the situation in Iran. This indicates that the Revolutionary Guard has become the heart of the country, seeking to impose its ideological and military doctrine upon society and the army. The Supreme Leader supports the Guard's military doctrine by appointing Guard leaders as commanders of the army and as defense ministers. The Guard has been the dominant intelligence and political organization in Iran in recent years,[30] reflecting the doctrine of the state and presenting it as the compass of Iran's strategic doctrine. Currently, the Revolutionary Guard is not only a guard of the revolution but also an active player, protector, and implementer of the revolutionary principles as well as the evaluator of political loyalty.[31]

The Pasdaranisation of the regime and the country progressed through many stages. Initially, during the revolutionary upheaval that overthrew the Shah, officers in the army were overthrown as well, forced into retirement or executed by the revolutionary courts. The new politicians changed many organizational structures of the regular forces. In addition, the regime embarked upon a massive campaign of Islamization of the armed forces through the ideological and political commission that Khomeini formed. The regime also changed the nature of the army's ideology[32] by instilling the new regime's values into the hearts and minds of its soldiers and leaders.[33] The ideological commission initiated sectarian education and political awareness for the soldiers and worked to develop a military organization inspired by the spirit of the doctrine, thereby reinforcing the concept of the ideological army and consolidating the Supreme Leader's authority. It uprooted anti-revolution feelings and ensured that the armed forces remained responsible to the political leadership.[34]

Above all, the army leadership underwent an intensive course of indoctrination and Islamic upbringing that the religious commissioners monitored. Until the mid1980-s, the army suffered from continuous purges. Estimates are that as many as 17,000 officers, representing 45% of all military officers, were victims of these purges through 1986.[35] Although this effort did not instill revolutionary concepts in the armed forces, it uprooted any possible anti-revolutionary sentiment and ensured that the army remained under the supervision of the political leadership.[36]

On the other hand, the Guard carried out political, ideological, and cultural indoctrination through the Political Bureau, which offered ideological, philosophical, and military lectures. The bureau helped promote and consolidate the Guard's ideology, as well as the office of the Supreme Leader's representative within the Guard. This representative is the main channel of indoctrination and is responsible for disseminating the Supreme Leadership theory. The office has emerged as a permanent force in organizing the Guard and is now responsible for the website and monthly magazine Sobhe-e Sadegh.[37] From this core, the Revolutionary Guard's ideological approach evolved into a network of cultural activities, institutes, intellectual centers, and youth camps abroad. Many of these activities take place alongside the activities of other entities, such as the Islamic Republic of Iran Radio (IRIB), the Ministry of Culture and Islamic Guidance, and the Islamic Propaganda Organization. Some of these institutions are headed and staffed by former Revolutionary Guard personnel.[38]

In addition to managing cultural awareness and indoctrination efforts, the Revolutionary Guard and the Basij have become deeply rooted in the Iranian education system at the university and secondary school levels.[39] In contrast to the army, which preferred to stay away from elite conflicts, the Guard has been closely linked to a number of "hawks" in the elite of the Iranian leadership, and has viewed itself primarily as a political army defending the revolution of Khomeini and its doctrine of supporting Muslims oppressed everywhere in the world.[40] The Guard infiltrated the army by establishing offices belonging to the Basij inside the army bases. As a result, membership in the Basij became a method that military officers employed to gain promotion in the military ranks. In 1992, the Office of the Joint Chief of Staff and the General Commander of the Armed Forces was established, placing the army and the Guard under joint command. However, competition and the distribution of roles remain clear, and within the Guard remains the sense that the army is less enthusiastic about its revolutionary and militant doctrine. The media leaked a statement from Strategic Analyst Hassan Abbasi, who has close ties to the Guard, explicitly describing the army as useless and silent without acting on domestic issues.[41]

The army was, and remains, a military organization operating according to a classical professional doctrine, while the Revolutionary Guard was, and still is, operating according to a doctrine of asymmetrical and "revolutionary" war.[42] Although the regime's official policy divided the duties between the army and the Guard, this policy was rarely followed. The Guard became the dominant player in the military apparatus, and its doctrine spread to the various organs, institutions, and ministries, whether through the presence of members belonging to the Supreme Leader and Guard or through values implanted by members of the Supreme Leadership and the Ministry of Culture and Islamic Propaganda. Some members of the Ministry of Culture and the Ministry of Internal Security belong to the Supreme Leader and to the brigades of the Revolutionary Guard.[43] The Guard's duties have been broadened horizontally and vertically to include the dissemination of Islamic morals, maintenance of internal security, exporting the revolution, overseeing of the economy, and engaging in military manufacturing. The Guard continues its ideological indoctrination and maintains the organizational, cultural, and religious structure that made it an independent, powerful institution of a special nature.[44] The indicator of state Pasdaranisation involves not only the Guard's domination over the country's doctrine but also practical indicators, such as the ascendance of one of its members (Mahmoud Ahmadinejad) to the presidency and the appointment of several ministers (as well as ambassadors and dozens of parliamentary deputies) from among the Guard.[45] A strong alliance was established between the Guard and the Supreme Leadership institution; the Guard merged into the theocratic institution, and a symbiotic relationship was established between the two.[46] Disagreements exist about the nature of the Guard's relationship with the Supreme Leader; some see it as a relationship governed by mutual need, while others believe the Guard has an influential presence within the institution and that its behavior reflects the Supreme Leader's views, making it a hostage of the Supreme Leader.[47] Still others see it as a relationship governed by the Guard's subsidiarity. According to Avshon Ostofar, "The Revolutionary Guards are the defenders of the guide, who blesses them with their holy names, allows them to demonize their enemies, and enables them to encapsulate their struggle with the Zoroastrian concepts about good and evil universally. Their activities are sly, very precise, and full of political trappings, aimed at preserving the revolutionary flame in the soul."[48]

Thus, the nature of the Iranian military doctrine changed completely so that it was the doctrine of the Revolutionary Guard, to the point that one of its leaders, General Qasem Soleimani, commander of the Quds Force in the Guard, claimed that "without the Revolutionary Guards there will be no homeland"![49] This led to complaints among many leaders and officials, including President Rouhani, who said that the Guard is a "state within the state" after its leaders continued engaging in economic and regime affairs.[50]

Third: Principles of external expansion in the doctrine of the Revolutionary Guard

The "employment interpretation" provides an appropriate analytical framework for extending the Guard's military doctrine inside and outside Iran. This interpretation attributes the developments in the military doctrine, which led to the dominance of the Guard's doctrine, to a target of survival and a postponing of internal conflict. The application of the Guard's doctrine represents an internal battle because many, if not most, of the Revolutionary Guard commanders, along with revolutionary leaders such as Khomeini, have struggled to ensure Iran's territorial integrity. Also, its application represents an opportunity to consolidate the revolution and its institutions and purge from them well-known and expected opponents.[51] Relatively, theories referring to the "search for an enemy" and the "creation of an enemy abroad" explain the expansionist principles in the Revolutionary Guard's doctrine abroad. Upon the expansion of the Guard's function over the decades (a result of this objective of expansionism), several elements and institutions were created to support the Guard and subsequently benefitted from the loops of influence and interest. Currently, after reaching the nuclear agreement with the West, it must reproduce the role by seeking another enemy.

The Iranian regime harbors great hostility. Its structure stems from the goal of unloading itsenergy in the struggle against claimed arrogant forces. If it does not find an arrogant force elsewhere in the world, it will find one in its neighboring countries. The end of conflict means the exposure of the regime and its dysfunctional system; thus, as its battle with the world decreases, its battle in the region increases and vice versa. The external threat for the sake of the country's survival has been a means of preventing the people from focusing on internal failure. This perception of danger and threat has deepened the people's mobilization behind the Revolutionary Guard and has reinforced the "Basij culture" in each geographical, economic, and communitarian sector in Iran.[52] This was confirmed by one of the Rand Foundation's studies, which affirmed that Iran's global strategic vision appears to be ideological and revolutionary but tends toward political realism,[53] or it fluctuates between utilitarianism and ideology in determining national interests.[54] If the Guard's forces are confined within the country's boundaries, it will incite internal conflicts between the various regime actors, creating more costs and burdens. Thus, intervention in crises abroad is pursued as a means of absorbing the tendency towards internal conflict. This is consistent with the regime's desire to distract Iranians from internal problems by sending a message that "the countries of the region witness chaos and political turmoil, and we must protect our borders and prevent these infections moving to us, so we can counter any internal opposition movements or manifestations of concern."[55] Thus, the practice of violence and the exportation of crises to neighboring countries is a deliberate move on the part of the regime –a move that ensures the regime's survival by requiring it to curb internal discontent and mobilize for external defense.[56] In light of this, a predicament exists that can be called "the dilemma of having to depart." This involves the urgent institutional need to rush forward due to the negative products stemming from the revolutionary state's practices for nearly 40 years, which have resulted in a "closed cycle" of crises. In this context, Maryam Rajavi, leader of the Iranian opposition, stresses that aggression in "the behavior of the Iranian regime is a tool for survival, but now it is floundering in the quagmire of war. It cannot progress, and it is in trouble now and there is no power to retreat, because it is between worse and the worst, if it retreated, it will lead to a faster collapse, and if it continues its stream, it will lose its capabilities and components completely."[57] According to Rajavi, the regime does this to stay in power; its actions in this respect have nothing to do with beliefs and the role of sectarianism. In September 2017, the Supreme Leader ordered the establishment of a new regulatory commission that will hold all governmental commissions accountable for their policies.[58] As a part of efforts to practice the Guard's regional expansionist objective, several principles and foundations have been developed in recent years, namely:

The first principle: Proactive war and transferring battles to enemy territory: The Quds Force, which was founded in the early 1990s, is the primary tool for achieving that goal and for supporting the Revolutionary Guard's general influence outside Iran's borders through military, political, and economic tools (as the Guards takes care of the financing and equipping process).[59] This fact is reflected in the words of the Republic Supreme Leader, Ali Khamenei, who said that the Iranian army soldiers who were killed in Syria in defense of Bashar al-Assad fell "in order to seize the fight within Iranian borders," and that "if we did not deter the wicked and the advocates of sedition from the agents of America and Zionism in Syria, we will face them in Tehran, Persia, Khorasan and Isfahan." Iran has applied this doctrine so that its army becomes more capable of launching sub-conventional war hundreds of miles from its borders. Iranian military commanders have rotated all branches of their forces – such as the Revolutionary Guard, the army, and the Basij – in Syria to involve and train a large proportion of Syrian forces in operations, tactics, and war. At the same time, Iranian military planners have redirected the traditional forces' technique for defense operations to create a reconnaissance force capable of conducting operations abroad for the first time since the end of the Iran-Iraq war.[60] Khamenei has attacked opponents of this strategy, insisting on the need to "suppress the enemy at its borders." On December 2016,6, he praised the dead of the so-called "defenders of Ahl al-Bayt shrine" who fell in Syria. He said, "They sacrificed themselves there so that the enemies would not reach the country, and without them we would not have to confront the enemies in Kermanshah, Hamdan and the rest of Iran's provinces."[61] According to Qasem Soleimani, the commander of the Quds Force of the Revolutionary Guard, Iran does not seek to profit from its interference in neighboring countries, but rather to protect itself and the Iranian people from the cholera and plague prevalent in the countries surrounding it. He said, "We have to impose quarantine on our borders, and all the passersby around us, we have to help the country infected with this disease, this way we protect ourselves."[62] This is the same explanation that many of the army's leaders give, citing the military principle that the best defense is attack, as expressed by Colonel Ahmed Glampour, a former Revolutionary Guard commander, who said that "through these strategies set by the Supreme Leader [Khamenei] Tehran was able to distance the confrontation with the enemy thousands [of] kilometers from the center of the Islamic Revolution (Iran)."[63] This principle embodies the belief in the doctrine of "pre-emptive war," which means anticipating threats abroad before they emerge and practicing war in neighboring countries as a means of removing threats to the center.

The second principle: The establishment of an Iranian orbit and the transformation into a regional superpower: Assisted by the significant change in the strategic environment, Iran has transformed from a country fearing a US strategic blockade after the invasion of Afghanistan (2001) and Iraq (2003) to a country that practices encirclement against Gulf countries. Iran is a stable country in the region, dominating Syria and Iraq, and a country whose preferred means of exerting influence has been "soft power." However, it has become a country that seeks a strategy using "soft and hard" capabilities, and that has gone from being a rogue nuclear country to standing on the threshold of fulfilling its nucleardream.[64]

Iran's goal of being a regional superpower becomes evident through its quest to impose hegemony and build a self-defense fence that enhances the usual pattern of Iranian interference in the affairs of neighboring countries, such as Iraq, Afghanistan, Syria, Saudi Arabia, Bahrain, and Kuwait in different forms and patterns. The level of Iranian regional intervention varies, but it is consistent with Iran's objective of seeking self-protection by interfering in weak countries standing under its sectarian um- brella, thus allowing it to become the first "regional" force in the Middle East. This goal was explicitly set out in Iran's 20-year strategy, endorsed by the Supreme Leader in 2014.[65] In addition, Iran is pursuing far-reaching changes on the regional and global stage to overcome the American blockade by courting various in- ternational partners.[66] In recent years, Iranian tools to infiltrate neighbors have not been limited to political, economic, ideolog- ical, and cultural tools or agent wars. The Revolutionary Guard has made direct military breakthroughs in the distressed states; thus, close integration of the goals of Iran's foreign policy and the doctrine of the Revolutionary Guard has emerged. Essentially, foreign policy has primarily served the Guard's practice, and the Guard has given the main impetus to Iranian policy. This means that a great deal of integration exists among the Guards, the in- stitutions of the Supreme Leader, and the Foreign Ministry. Such a fact becomes clear when one considers the Supreme Leader's decision to assign Guard leadership to foreign missions and con- sultations. These decisions regarding appointments are not in the hands of the Foreign Ministry or President Rouhani himself, which obstructs citizens' knowledge of foreign policy develop- ment.[67] Iran's ambition is to control the Middle East, led by the Special Operation Forces of the Revolutionary Guard, by coop- erating with a variety of Sunni extremist organizations that also promote this ambition. One aspect of this cooperation was the Iranian Revolutionary Guard's training of affiliated organizations that could help achieve Iran's foreign policy goals. This was seen earlier when the Islamic Republic trained Sunni and Shiite fight- ers who supported Iran's foreign policy objectives, as thousands of trainees passed through this system.[68] The Quds Force's Corps of the Revolutionary Guard is divided into specific groups accord- ing to each country's geographic division. The Corps has offices in several Iranian embassies abroad. The Quds Force's external branches are divided into commissions according to the fields in which they operate: guerrilla and urban warfare, and asymmetric warfare.[69] Moreover, it has the authority to carry out any military action outside Iran's borders without informing the Iranian gov- ernment or other agencies. It follows the Supreme Leader directly without interference from the Iranian government, and its budget deficit is recovered by the "House of Khamenei" or any part of the Supreme Leader's budget.[70] However, Foreign Minister Javad Zarif has mentioned this strategy repeatedly within his participa- tion in American agencies and intellectual organizations. Iran's interventions beyond its borders stem from the Revolutionary Guard's ambition to transform the Islamic Republic into a region- al superpower, while the "moderates" prefer only to build "mutu- ally advantageous relations" with the West.[71]

The third principle: Sectarian jihad, the sectarian nature of wars, and sectarian armies: Reliance on sectarian parties in countries with Shiite minorities has been a continuous stream in Iranian military doctrine since the revolution of 1979 and has been practiced in Lebanon in the form of its experience with Hezbollah. The experience of Iran and the Revolutionary Guard in Iraq and then Syria has caused these countries to become bases of Iranian military doctrine, which involves relying on sectarian jihadist groups and organizations in the countries under intervention to support the Revolutionary Guard's incursions.[72] This model of war management is the latest version of the military, similar to what the Basij enacted during the Iran-Iraq war. In that war, the Basij was the main military force that trained youth and even the elderly in mosques; these trained forces then attacked enemy defense positions, cleaned minefields, and carried out mass offensive waves to facilitate the safe advancement of the armed forces, which were directly behind them.[73]

Iran's doctrine of sectarian mobilization and the sectarian na- ture of its warmongering is connected to its desire to build an Iranian jurisdiction for

Shiites, regardless of their homelands. According to Adel al-Jubeir, the Saudi foreign minister at the Mu- nich security conference, Tehran does not believe in the concept of citizenship but prioritizes affiliation with the Iranian Republic whether or not the person is an Iranian citizen.[74] This Iranian ap- proach has become more prevalent in recent years, with active Iranian efforts to weaken and infiltrate neighboring countries through espionage, violent cells, and provocative statements. It was not surprising that, in November 2016, a close associate of the Supreme Leader Khamenei announced the seizure of four Arab capitals. Nor was it surprising that the Deputy Commander of the Revolutionary Guards, Major General Hussein Salami, said that "victory in Aleppo is an introduction to the liberation of Bah- rain."[75] Similarly, some sources point out that more than 20 Shiite factions fighting in Syria were linked to Iran and the Revolution- ary Guard through mid-2014.[76] These Shiite organizations are involved in the Revolutionary Guard's military doctrine as sup- porting groups that reduce the losses of the Guard and Iran in its regional wars. The most dangerous aspect is that fighters return- ing from Syria, Iraq, and Afghanistan could create new challenges for the region and the Gulf countries.[77]

The fourth principle: Revolutionary Guard cloning and disseminating the guerilla warfare model: One of the Rev- olutionary Guard's military doctrine objectives is to clone and construct military and paramilitary clusters for countries in cri- sis. This explains the concept of unconventional warfare behind enemy lines, guerrilla warfare carried out by sectarian masses, rather than direct intervention, with a wide range of "non-state" forces and jihadists in the broader Shiite world. The principle of dumping the enemy into a quagmire of unconventional warfare is a fundamental Iranian one, and is supported by a study from the American War College titled "Vulnerabilities exploited by the Iranian Revolutionary Guards," which mentioned that "one of the major facts about the IRG's doctrine is the idea of relying on unconventional and unfamiliar wars for other regular armies to compensate for the lack of technological and combat capabilities in Iran. The idea of unconventional warfare is to defeat the will of the stronger party and to reduce its enthusiasm to continue fight- ing instead of militarily confrontation by conventional means." In addition, the study mentioned: "To achieve this, Iran can rely on the non-existence of a centralized central command for its forces and the distribution of its units on the ground to overcome the usual air superiority of its enemies."[78] The commander-in-chief of the Revolutionary Guard, Major General Mohammad Ali Jafari, has revealed the presence of about 200,000 fighters associated with the Revolutionary Guard in Syria, Iraq, Yemen, Afghanistan, and Pakistan and said he is looking forward to encouraging the third generation of the revolution to support the Supreme Lead- ership and the Iranian Republic in Iran, pointing out the impor- tance of young Iranians' involvement in the battles of Syria, Iraq, and Yemen.[79] The principle of cloning the Guard model and ex- porting its project is being implemented gradually in Iraq, Syria, Lebanon, Pakistan, and A fghanistan, as is Iran's normalizat ion with certain neighboring countries. This fact has been revealed in many reports that indicated the Revolutionary Guard, the Min- istry of Islamic Culture and Propaganda, and the Ministry of In- telligence and Internal Security exploited neighboring countries' weaknesses and provided decisive political, military, econo mic, humanitarian, and securi ty support.[80] This is reinforced by the relationship between the Guard's doctrine and economic inter- ests to sustain its defe nse doctrine. As a result, the Guard has gained status, influence, and wealth since the 1980s.[81] This situa- tion is strengthened by an increase in the Guard's budget despite the Iranian president's disapproval. An analysis of Iranian data about the various budgets, especially for 2017, indicates that the Guard's budget doubled.[82]

The fifth principle: The practice of terrorism in the military doctrine: Although the Revolutionary Guard is a branch of the army of the Iranian state, it plays an informal militia role and is involved in practicing terrorism. The practice of terrorism holds a special place in the Iranian government's military doctrine and its support for terrorism is closely linked to its regional goals.[83] In May 2004 Hussein Abbasi, head of the Center for Strategic and Ideological Studies at the Revolutionary Guards at Imam Hussain University, summarized the Revolutionary Guard's philosophy in terms of using and employing terrorism: "The Islamic world needs suicide bombings. I am one who is developing theories of terrorism and violence that shakes the infidelity base."[84] Iran has a history of targeted killings and mass bombings intended to remove the regime's main opponents or to send a political message. Notably, the Quds Force of the Revolutionary Guard carried out more than 30 foreign-country attacks between 2011 and 2013, including in Thailand, India, Nigeria, and Kenya. Also, it was involved in an attempted assassination of the Saudi Ambassador to the United States.[85]

It is obvious that the Guard has links with terrorist organiza- tions but, more importantly, it targets other countries and desta- bilizes them as part of its doctrine. This is codified in the Consti- tution in the guise of supporting the vulnerable and the Islamic resistance outside Iran's borders and defending the shrines of the Al-Bayt. These slogans cover many of the Guard's illegal activities. However, exporting terrorism and the promotion of war based on the Supreme Leader's vision are activities that self-motivate the Guard and the spirit that controls it.[86] Above all, Iranian military doctrine is clearly concentrated in the Guard, which has the up- per hand in terms of implementing this doctrine and drawing the general political alignment of the Iranian state, which no longer revolves around the revolution's ideology or the religious aspect, but rather is a sectarian political ideology leading to a vicious cir- cle of interest. It is inconceivable that a change will occur in the Guard's military doctrine without the interests and internal busi- ness cycles that benefit Guard commanders being shaken, due to the Guard's huge gains from its recent interventions. This was a sufficient reason for two presidents as different as Ahmadinejad and Rouhani to complain about the Guard. The former hinted at the Guard's involvement in smuggling, using the term "smuggled brothers."[87]

President Rouhani complained about the Guard's intervention in matters related to the country's economy, saying in his speech during the celebration of the Iranian Army Day in Tehran "The obsession of the armed forces in the economy of the country dis- tracts it from its objective, and removes its leaders and the armed forces from their original duties."[88] Rouhani repeated his criticism of the Guard; he later said that part of the economy was in the hand of the armless government and that the other part had been given to a government that owned the gun, adding that if inves- tors were afraid of a government that did not own a gun, what about a government that owned the economy.[89]

For their part, the Guard's leaders called for the task of econom- ic administration to be handed over to the Guard, claiming that the country's economic file was not properly managed, as stated by former Revolutionary Guard commander Mohsen Rezai.[90] The commander of the Guard, Mohammad Jafari, attacked Rouhani and accused him of abandoning "the implementation of the com- mitments that concern the lives of the people and the economy of Iran." He stressed that the Revolutionary Guard and the Basij were determined to compensate in any possible way for the im- balanced living conditions and to lessen Iran's economic woes, like its military role.[91] The military doctrine of the Iranian armed forces and the Revolutionary Guard transcends Iran's actual mili- tary capabilities. Since the Iran-Iraq war, the Iranian army has not been tested in a systematic war outside its border. So far, the Rev- olutionary Guard is engaged in guerrilla warfare in neighboring countries, which means that the Revolutionary Guard's arms are the regime's spearhead. The Guard's capabilities in terms of ex- pansion and penetration are stronger than the actual capabilities of Iran, which covers the weaknesses in Iran's actual armaments and capabilities. Therefore, an observer of the political discourse and the Iranian military is distracted by a mass of political state- ments from many military and political officials, emphasizing the Guard as the official military representative.

Fourth: The ambiguity involved in determining the "enemy."

Analyzing the enemy is one of the most important pillars of any country's military doctrine. This issue appears to be ambiguous in the Iranian military doctrine. For decades, Iran has been con- sidered a revolutionary country under the slogan of "the Great Satan and Israel." However, the level of armed activities or direct hostility on the part of Iran towards the two countries or vice ver- sa is not consistent with its exaggerated emphasis in Iran's mili- tary doctrine. Iran, on the other hand, involved itself in an eight- year war with Iraq and continued its violent espionage activities against Gulf State countries. The Iranian discourse implies a du- alism that makes the task of recognizing Iran's true enemy diffi- cult to achieve. The Iranian military doctrine has seen a deviation from the Guard's vision dominating the professional army. Hence, a particular ideology has been ingrained, founded on ideological grounds rather than on military professionalism and based on a broader assessment of Iran's national security threats. However, despite the ambiguity with respect to identifying the enemy in the Iranian military doctrine, in recent years the tone of Irani- an hostility towards arrogant global forces has diminished. The traditional Iranian discourse regarding the "Great Satan" and Is- rael is receding. The focus is now on the narrow circle that has, according to Iranian military doctrine, begun threatening Iran's national security. Generally, the Iranian leaders assert that "Iran's military capabilities are defensive and pose a threat to no one, especially our Arab neighbors. Rather, our military capabilities are not to defend Iran only, but all Muslim countries." In his April 18 National Army Day speech, President Rouhani described his country's military doctrine as "defensive," asserting that Iran's military strategy was based on "active deterrence to establish peace and security in Iran and the countries of the region." Irani- an officials point out that throughout history, Iran has not waged war against a foreign country, but has been the victim of foreign intervention and the imposition of foreign wars (for example, the invasion of Iraq in 1980). Iran's military policy does not believe in "the first strike principle."[92] Lately, Iranian officials have made regular hostile statements about the Gulf countries and Saudi Arabia in particular. This fact reinforces the sectarian and histor- ical inheritance influencing Iran's hostility towards the Kingdom and revealed in Iran's aggressive statements against the Kingdom. Such a fact was reflected in Iran's reaction to the Saudi-US deal during President Trump's visit to the Kingdom, as well as in Iran's position on the Gulf crisis with Qatar; Iran's bias towards Qatar's position was clearly visible. A former US ambassador, Fred Hoff, who held far-sighted meetings with Iranian officials, concluded that "his Iranian interlocutors unanimously agreed that the real enemy is Saudi Arabia." The Iranian Revolutionary Guard is an- gered about Riyadh's position against the Syrian revolution and its position concerning the situation in both Yemen and Iraq. This is reflected in the statement that the commander of the Guards, General Mohammad Ali Jafari, made on July 21, 2016; he said that Saudi Arabia was the "first enemy" of Iran.[93] There is a process of peaceful transformation to re-establish and embody the enemy of Iran, including primarily the Arab Gulf countries. This forces the Gulf countries to complain about the various forms of Iranian interference in their internal situations, whether via cells of vio- lence, espionage, or media meddling. It can be said that the Rev- olutionary Guard witnessed the greatest change in its qualitative doctrine through the Arab revolutions and the nuclear agreement with the West. Consequently, it considers Saudi Arabia to be its enemy while it reduces the tone of its hostility against America and Israel. This trend towards boosting hostility against Saudi Arabia is prevalent not only in Iran but also in the armed forc- es as represented by the army and the Revolutionary Guard, as well as in Iran's sectarian military institutions in other countries, such as Hezbollah. In many speeches, its leader, Hassan Nasrallah, has poured out his anger towards the Kingdom. One possibility is that Iran's escalation and the continuation of its threat against the Kingdom may be part of a tactical management strategy to nor- malize relations. This means that the hostility might not reflect the core of Iran's military doctrine. Between the hostile statements about the Kingdom and the Gulf countries and the internal divi- sion between those who hold an ideological view of the hostility and the pragmatists' desire to coexist, it is difficult to claim that the focus of Iran's national security doctrine has moved towards inevitable confrontation with the Kingdom. Although Iran's polit- ical, media, and military positions are not friendly and are hostile towards Saudi Arabia, it is difficult to find "institutional official documents" such as the "US National Security document," which considers Saudi Arabia as its first enemy. Likewise, it is difficult to claim that Iran's military doctrine is based on the possibility that Saudi Arabia will launch a military attack against the Iranian Republic or adjust its military industries and defense purchases to confront any expected Saudi military strike. In general, the net- work of enemies, according to Iran's vision, has prevented it from establishing a typical hostile position towards one enemy. Saudi Arabia is seen as a selective enemy at a specific time, but not for the long run.

Ultimately, it can be said that under the current status of the armed forces and the discrepancy between the military doctrine of the army and the Revolutionary Guard, the following interac- tion and operation scenarios between the two doctrines can be expected as the time of a threat is assumed, as follows:

First: In the case of internal turmoil and rebellion, or revolu- tion in Iran, it is expected that the army will not interfere and that it will not be assigned any military task unless the senior leader- ship asks for this. That is why the Revolutionary Guard is inca- pable of resolving unrest. Accordingly, the army's intervention is not intended to protect the regime, but to protect the country and the nation, as its faith is not grounded in protecting the Islamic Republic.

Second: A war with Iran and an attack on Iran in reaction to the Guard's intervention in neighboring countries may plausibly call for a military reaction from the army, as its duty is to defend the country. Thus, it will be affected by the consequences of the Guard's policies abroad. This would be the matching point be- tween the doctrine of the army and the Guard. Thus, despite the army's independence, it would maintain a role in responding to the Guard's crises, even if such an act would be against its will.

Third: If the Guard's ideology controls the military doctrine of the armed forces and the political doctrine of Iran, this dom- inance may decline if the Guard experiences a setback abroad and if a green revolution is repeated or dissent arises.[94] The same applies if a change is made in the ruling composition, thereby af- fecting the institution of the Supreme Leadership, which will re- main on the same principles as Khamenei.[95] Here, the Supreme Leadership, which will follow Khamenei's principles, may resort to balancing the Guard's strength as a means of restoring the ef- fectiveness of the professional army's doctrine at the expense of the Revolutionary Guard's doctrine.

Fifth: A strategy to dismantle the Guard's military doctrine

Above all, the Revolutionary Guard has become one of the tools involved in the implementation of Iran's military and stra- tegic doctrine and the most important player in achieving it. The Guard's strategic doctrine has become the spearhead in the state's political doctrine. Therefore, it is difficult to imagine that a change will be made in the regime's military doctrine before a change is made in the Revolutionary Guard's military doctrine. Clearly, the economy is a fundamental dimension in the face of Iran's mili- tary doctrine ;the Guard's heightened practices in neighboring countries accompany an increase in oil revenues and the return of frozen assets. It is also clear that the Iranian armed forces 'in- volvement in partial and guerrilla wars does not indicate the to- tal strength of Iran's military capabilities. Therefore, in dealing with the special case of Iran's military doctrine and its practices through the Revolutionary Guard, one can imagine the following points. These points are mainly the conception of an" asymmet- ric "strategy for dismantling the Guard's role and its doctrine. The central question one can ask is: Can the existence of the current Iranian regime and its policies be tolerated ?The answer is no. The second question is: Is confrontation with Iran the choice ?In- deed, this would prolong internal militarization, which is an ideal situation for the Guard's leaders to continue their intervention in neighboring countries and to promote the persistence of the Supreme Leader's extremism. This means that a militaristic and ideological discourse would continue dominating Iranian society. In addition, military confrontation and war would have negative consequences, and the adoption of a new Shiite oppressor would dominate the memory of all Shiites in the region for a long time. A war with Iran would mean that the regime would continue for a more extended period, as would the Guard's military doctrine, due to the fact that more popular and social bases would be be- hind it. This would be the most substantial blow to the forces of reform and change inside Iran. It would also increase the number of individuals who support militarization and the revolutionary ideology as well as empower Shiite jihadist campaigns with their destructive capabilities. Additional military preparation would be necessary to confront the numerous organizations proliferat-ing versions of the Revolutionary Guard in the region. Therefore, it is crucial to create a strategy that would lead to internal change in Iran without war, based on a careful reading of the power bal- ance and its transformations in Iran. The strategy's most essen-tial elements for facing this situation, if an opportunity exists for negotiation, dialogue, or regional accountability with Iran, are as follows:

a. **Focusing on normalizing institutions' statuses from in- side before outside:** This would normalize relations with Iran by normalizing the conditions of its military institutions and dis- mantling its military and political doctrine, which is based on sec- tarian, political, and military hostility towards the Gulf countries, as well as by linking economic development to demilitarization. The aim is to confront and overthrow the Guard's ideology, not to overthrow the Iranian regime. If this happens, the result would likely be a major internal transformation in Iran and, by exten- sion, the defeat of extremism at home, the driving of Iran out of its military dictatorship doctrine, the dismantling of control over the Iranian mind, and the removal of state oppression. This ef- fort could be promoted by exploiting dissatisfaction towards the Revolutionary Guard's policies at home, thereby supporting in- ternal change in Iran, accompanied by the Iranian army's role in countering the Guard's role. Furthermore, the effort could involve returning Iran's military doctrine to a balance between the Guard and the army or pushing it to a point where the army – not the Revolutionary Guard – is the center of the military doctrine.

b. **Helping to gradually change the militarization situation:** The act of facing the deviation of the military doctrine of the Rev- olutionary Guard should be based on dismantling and disarming it without using the military machine. This can be accomplished by working to change Iranian society so that Iran is removed from the militarization situation that the regime reinforces. Here, it is possible to work with the opposition at home and with millions of Iranians abroad. However, weakening public support for the Guard's doctrine requires lessening the Guard's role by monitor- ing its economic dealings and reducing its role at home. This move would be aimed at "dismantling Iran intellectually and politically" and disconnecting economic dealings with it to gain the support of parties inside Iran, which may constitute the most significant bloc regarding dismantling this military doctrine. In Iran, multiple social classes stand with the region in its desire to see a different Iran. Recognition exists that this strategy to peacefully change Iran may last two decades and require supporting the forces of change for gradual and automatic development.

c. **Continuing the confrontation, in non-military forms, with the Revolutionary Guard's doctrine:** This would be done by highlighting the extreme nature of the Guard's doctrine in vari- ous international forums as part of an international campaign tar- geting it. This strategy requires focusing on the legal perspective and classifying Iran's actual practices as illegal, as well as stipu- lating that no difference exists among the Revolutionary Guard, Al-Qaeda, and ISIS except that the Revolutionary Guard carries out its activities under the cloak of the Iranian state. The main ob- jective would be to create a picture of the Revolutionary Guard as being similar to Al-Qaeda and other fascist organizations, seeking to drain Iran economically in its imperial expansion (Iraq, Syria, Lebanon, and Yemen). This would force the Guard to retreat from the scene, so that the Iranian army, with its traditional national professional doctrine, could organize Iran's military doctrine. Ac- companying this would be the adoption of a strategy against Revo- lutionary Guard-linked Shiite jihadist organizations and the pros- ecution of its proxies, similar to the Arab encirclement of Qatar and Sunni terrorist groups.

d. **Engaging in asymmetrical war through the economy and development:** The Iranian military doctrine is based on guerrilla warfare; therefore, it is important to find a military doctrine for the GCC countries to counter and paralyze this guerrilla warfare. The GCC can achieve this because of the finite nature of Iran's capabili- ties. The Iranian military faces structural and organizational prob- lems that prevent Tehran from pursuing its ideological ambitions for asymmetric war; these problems are likely to continue over the next five to ten years.[96] In light of this fact, as an essential aspect of the strategy to confront Iran, the GCC countries must focus on raising their standards of living, developing their economies, and maintaining their people's prosperity. This is a constructive strat- egy that would mitigate the power of the Iranian regime's tricks in continuing its ideological statements against the GCC in front of its people. Also, the GCC countries must not collide with Iran (and its armed, doctrinal, and ideological networks) in symmetrical war- fare that could destroy the infrastructure and economic structures that the GCC countries have built for decades while, simultaneous- ly, Iran would have nothing to lose. Therefore, the best strategy is to direct GCC countries to widen the gap between competition and development and to balance their prosperity with respect to Iran. The GCC countries must also defeat Iran in non-military areas as a means of proving that Iran lacks ability in these areas. This is the model of war upon which the United States relied to defeat and disintegrate the Soviet Union in the early 1990s. Similarly, the social, economic, and political modernization processes taking place in GCC countries, such as the NEOM and Red Sea projects in the Kingdom, and the Path of Hope and the Louvre Museum in the UAE, are examples of asymmetrical warfare that can create a gap between the Iranian regime and its people. This clarifies the differ- ence between a traditional regime that seeks to spread and nour- ish the culture of martyrdom and the destruction of neighboring countries and regimes that seek to modernize their societies vig- orously and to promote a culture of tolerance and the right to life and prosperity. Through this strategy, the continuous pressure on the nerves of the Iranian regime will lead to an "Iranian spring" that develops quietly and achieves the desired purpose without the need for sorties or shooting.

Endnotes

(1) The Artesh: Iran's Marginalized Regular Military. Middle East Institute Viewpoints. November 10 .2011. https://www.mei.edu/sites/default/files/publications/2011.11. The20%Artesh20%Full20%PDF.pdf.

(2) Wege, Carl Anthony. "Iran's Intelligence Establishment." Journal of U.S. Intelligence Studies 21, no. 2 (Summer 65: (2015.

(3) The Artesh: Iran's Marginalized Regular Military, Op. cit. 16-9.

(4) Katzman, Kenneth. Iranian Revolutionary Guard: Its Origins, Composition and Role (Translated Studies 3). United Arab Emirates: Emirates Center for Strategic Studies and Research, 41-40 .1998.

(5) See the Iranian Constitution at the following link: https://www.constituteproject.org/ constitution/Iran_1989.pdf?lang=en

(6) Salama, Mu>taz. "The Army and Revolutionary Guard." International Politics 33, no. 130, (October 81: (1997.

(7) Bar, Shmuel. Iranian Terrorist Policy and "Export of Revolution". Proceedings of The Ninth Annual Herzliya Conference on the Balance of Israel's National Security and Resilience. Interdisciplinary Center (IDC) Herzliya, Lauder School of Government, Diplomacy and Strategy, Institute for Policy and Strategy, 2 .2009.

(8) McInnis, J. Matthew. Iranian Concepts of Warfare, Understanding Tehran's Evolving Military Doctrines. American Enterprise Institute. February 1 .2017.

(9) Bar, Smuel. Iranian Defense Doctrine and Decision Making. The Interdisciplinary Center Herzliya, Lauder School of Government, Diplomacy and Strategy, Institute for Policy and Strategy. 2004. i.

(10) Wehrey, Frederic et al. Dangerous But Not Omnipotent, Exploring the Reach and Limitations of Iranian Power in the Middle East. Project Air Force. Rand. 2009. 11.

(11) Idris, Mohammad Sayed. Iran and Arab National Security. Arab Center for Research and Policy Studies. January 2011,17. http://www.dohainstitute.org/release/-33849406 856c-4834-ac-21ce38b0074ae7.

(12) Bar, Shmuel. Iranian Terrorist Policy, Op. cit. 10-4.

(13) McInnis, J. Matthew. Iranian Concepts of Warfare, Op. cit. 1.

(14) Bar, Shmuel. Iranian Defense Doctrine and Decision Making, Op. cit. 57.

(15) Lewis, Patrick. Asymmetry of Will: The Effect of Religious Radicalism on State Military Doctrine. Master's thesis, The Massachusetts Institute of Technology. Boston: Boston College, 57-56. 2012.

(16) See: Samuel, Annie Tracy. Perceptions and Narratives of Security: The Iranian Revolutionary Guards Corps and the Iran-Iraq War. Belfer Center for Science and International Affairs, John F. Kennedy School of Government, Harvard University. May 2012. https://www.belfercenter.org/sites/default/files/legacy/files/samuel_ perceptions.pdf.

(17) Ibid., 6.

(18) For example, in one of the army and Revolutionary Guard's military reviews in the presence of Supreme Leader Ali Khamenei, the soldiers sang a collective chant with a single voice to the military music, in which Allah, Akbar Allah Akbar, says: "Our souls are a sacrifice for our leader... with divine breaths... Malicious plans have crashed. As you stood firmly and straight in front of the lions... Plans of evil destroyed... You are the origin of the light... The spirit of love... Inside us your love light... Rose of roses... O Muhammad, O Messenger of Allah... next to the great leader Khamenei... We are Jafari doctrine and thought. Thank God... Thank God... Because we are Haidarioun... we love our Leader... and loyal to Imam Ali... O Abu Zahra... O Muhammad, O Messenger of Allah. I am Basijion... Haidarion... You, O Ali is our leader. You are the meaning of our duties... Sayed Ali (Khamenei) our leader. Our martyrs... our pride. We will never back down. We are committed to your memory... O Muhammad, O Messenger of Allah. Watch the video at the following link:
https://www.youtube.com/watch?v=e2B2QfvDJnA&t=29s

(19) The Revolutionary Guard and the Basij organize regular training and exercises for active and potential Basijis, separate from the place of living or social class. These courses include theoretical and practical lessons. The exercises have four functions: training members to defend the homeland, offering disaster relief, preparing the Basijis to defend the regime and face

a possible "soft coup," and seizing the opportunity to assert allegiance to the Pasadaran and create the "Basij spirit."
See: Martonosi, Peter. "The Basij, A Major Factor in Iranian Security." AARMS 11, no.,1 32-30: (2012).

(20) McInnis, J. Matthew. Iran's Strategic Thinking, Origins and Evolution. American Enterprise Institute. May 2015. iii.

(21) Martonosi, Peter. "The Basij." Op. cit. 33-32.

(22) For additional details, see Massad, Nevin Abdel Moneim. Decision Making in Iran and Arab-Iranian Relations. Beirut: Center for Arab Unity Studies, 139-137 .2001.

(23) The Artesh: Iran's Marginalized Regular Military, Op. cit. 35-34.

(24) Al-Arimi, Rashid. "Revolutionary Guards Face the Real Iran." Al-Hayat. March 2013,6.

(25) Buchta, Wilfried. Who Rules Iran? The Structure of Power in the Islamic Republic: A Joint Publication of The Washington Institute for Near East Policy and the Konrad Adenauer Stiftung. Washington: The Washington Institute for Near East Policy, 67 .2000. https://www.washingtoninstitute. org/uploads/Documents/pubs/WhoRulesIran.pdf.

(26) Byman, Daniel et al. Iran's Security Policy in the Post-Revolutionary Era. RAND, .2001 33.

(27) Buchta, Wilfried. Who Rules Iran? Op. cit. 66-65.

(28) Talebi, Shahla & Saeid Golkar. "Captive Society: The Basij Militia and Social Control in Iran." Journal of the Society for Contemporary Thought and the Islamicate World. March 2016,29. http://www.sctiw.org/yahoo_site_admin/ assets/docs/102_Captive_Society_ Shahla_Talebi.87172344.pdf

(29) Buchta, Wilfried. Who Rules Iran? Op. cit. 67.

(30) Banerjea, Udit. "Revolutionary Intelligence: The Expanding Intelligence Role of the Iranian Revolutionary Guard Corps." Journal of Strategic Security 8, no. 105 .2015 .3.

(31) Dobbins, James et al. Coping With a Nuclearizing Iran, National Security Research Division. RAND, 21 .2011.

(32) Byman, Daniel et al. Iran's Security Policy, Op. cit. 32.

(33) "Iranian Military." The University of Texas at Austin. https://www. strausscenter.org/ hormuz/iranian-military.html.
Also: Amount, Hala Rashid. "The Iranian Constitution Episode 3-3: Armed Forces Arm of Oppressive Regime. Special Situation and Huge Budget." Middle East. January 2016,11.

(34) Wehrey, Frederic et al. The Rise of the Pasdaran. Op. cit. 2.

(35) Buchta, Wilfried. Who Rules Iran? Op. cit. 68.

(36) Byman, Daniel et al. Iran's Security Policy. Op. cit. 32.

(37) Wehrey, Frederic et al. The Rise of the Pasdaran. Op. cit. 36.

(38) 38- Ibid., 37.

(39) See: Ibid., 44-38.

(40) Buchta, Wilfried. Who Rules Iran? Op. cit. p 68.

(41) "Tehran Boasts: We Employ Our Experience in Yemen, Syria, Iraq and Lebanon, on the 36th Anniversary of the First Gulf War." Al-Sharq Al-Awsat. September 2016,22.

(42) See: The Artesh: Iran's Marginalized Regular Military, Op. cit. 33.

(43) Iranian Military, Op. cit.

(44) Katzman, Kenneth. Iranian Revolutionary Guards. Op. cit. 25-22.

(45) The Vandal Role of the Iranian Revolutionary Guard Corps in the Middle East. The European Association for the Freedom of Iraq and the International Commission for the Search for Justice. March 3 .2017. http://www.albasrah. net/ar_articles_0317/2017/ dor_tkhribi_270317.pdf

(46) Banerjea, Udit. "Revolutionary Intelligence." Op. cit. 106.

(47) Al-Nuaimi, Huda. Revolutionary Guards... Iran's Foreign Arm. Center of Links. July,9 2012. http://rawabetcenter.com/archives/56.

(48) See: Roberts, Mark. "Vanguard of the Imam: Religion, Politics, and Iran's Revolutionary Guards. By Afshon Ostovar." Journal of Strategic Security 9, no. 2. Summer 133 .2016.

(49) Taheri, Amir. "Rouhani and Trump: Together in the Face of the Revolutionary Guard?" Middle East. July 2007.

(50) President Hassan Rouhani strongly criticized the Guard's role in the fields of the economy, media, and politics, calling him "the parallel government carrying a gun." On the other hand, the response of Qasem Soleimani, the senior commander of the Revolutionary Guard and the head of the Quds Force, to the Guards harshly criticized Rouhani. Soleimani linked the existence of Iran to the presence of the Guard, saying: "Without the Guard there would be no country." See: "Soleimani Attacks Rouhani and Ties Iran›s Presence to the 'Guard.'" Middle East, July 2017,5. Former Iranian President Ahmadinejad had entered into a dispute with the Revolutionary Guard to the limit, pushing guards to accuse the group Mashayih, to which Ahmadinejad belonged, of a relationship with the Western intelligence apparatus and the Masonic movement in light of the escalation of power between Ahmadinejad and his group, Supreme Leader Ali Khamenei, and the conservative front. See: "Iran›s Revolutionary Guards hammer a nail into the coffin of the Mahdawis: Ahmadinejad, Jew, and Masonic." Middle East Online. 2011/8/7 http://www.middle- east-online.com/? id=115488http3%A2%F2%Fwww. middle- east- online. com2%F3%Fid3%D115488.

(51) Wehrey, Frederic et al. The Rise of the Pasdaran. Op. cit. 25-24.

(52) Ibid., 32.

(53) Ibid., 8.

(54) McInnis, J. Matthew. Iran's Strategic Thinking, Op. cit. iii.

(55) Alsulami, Mohammed. "Iranian Fighting Abroad and Ways of Exposing Its Goals." Al- Watan Saudi Arabia. January 2017,26.

(56) Wehrey, Frederic et al., The Rise of the Pasdaran. Op. cit. 25.

(57) Special meeting with Maryam Rajavi, President of the Iranian Resistance on the fifth anniversary of the Syrian revolution, published on March 2016,18. https://www. youtube.com/watch?v=0Ew3boRmylU.

(58) Taheri, Amir. "Khamenei Establishes New Body to Impose Further Restrictions on Government." Middle East. September 2017,25.

(59) Zahran, Yousra. "Revolutionary Guards, Different Combat Doctrine, and (Al-Jaafari) is Password." Egyptian Nation. August 2015,27. http://www.elwatannews.com/news/ details/793639. The original study:
Corrigan, Sean J. Exploitable Vulnerabilities of Iran's Islamic Revolutionary Guard Corps. United States Army War College. 2011.

(60) Bucala, Paul. Iran's New Way of War in Syria. A Report by the Critical Threats Project of the American Enterprise Institute and the Institute for the Study of War. February,1 2017.

(61) "Khamenei: We fight in Syria So As Not to Be Fought Within Our Borders." Al Arabia Net. January 2017,5.

(62) "General Qasem Soleimani's Message to President Obama." YouTube. November,6 2015.
https://www.youtube.com/watch?v=LEjwBRWBSMs.

(63) "Iranian Leader: Khamenei Transferred the War to Syria and Yemen." Arab Net. October 2016,6.

(64) Eisenstadt, Michael. "The Strategic Culture of the Islamic Republic of Iran, Religion, Expediency, and Soft Power in an Era of Disruptive Change." MES Monographs, no. 7, (November 2: (2015.

(65) Taheri, Amir. Rouhani and Trump. Op. cit.

(66) Wehrey, Frederic et al. Dangerous But Not Omnipotent. Op. cit. iii- iv.

(67) "Khamenei Establishes a New Commission to Impose Further Restrictions on Government." Middle East. September 2017,25.

(68) Wege, Carl Anthony. "Iran's Intelligence Establishment." Op. cit. 66

(69) Alnuaimi, Huda. Revolutionary Guards... Iran's Foreign Arm. Op. cit.

(70) "Alsulami, Adel, Commander of Iran›s Revolutionary Guard, Admits 200 the Existence of Thousand Fighters in Five Countries in the Region." Middle East. January,14 2016.

(71) Taheri, Amir. Rouhani and Trump, Op. cit.

(72) For the practice of this policy in Iraq, see: Knights, Michael. "The Evolution of Iran's Special Groups in Iraq." CTC Sentinel 3, nos. 12-11 (November 15-12: (2010.

(73) Martonosi, Peter. "The Basij." Op. cit. 29.

(74) "The Most Dangerous Article in the Iranian Constitution." Al Arabiya.net. February 2017,19.

(75) Hamid, Saleh. "Revolutionary Guard: After Aleppo We Will Enter Bahrain and Yemen." Al Arabia Net. December 2016,16.

(76) See: "Shiite Militias in Syria. The Story With Blood and Numbers." Al-Arabia Net.
June 2014,9. Also: "Shiite Militias Fighting in Syria." http://sn4hr.org/public_html/wp- content / pdf / arabic / shia% 27a- arabic.pdf

(77) Beheiri, Ahmad Kamel. "The Coming Confrontation. Former Shiite from the Armed Organizations in Syria." Al-Ahram Evening, September 2017,13.

(78) Zahran, Yosra, "Revolutionary Guard, A Different Doctrine of Combat." Op. cit.

(79) Alsulami, Adel. "Commander of Iran's Revolutionary Guard Admits." Op. cit.

(80) Shafa, Reza. "Afghanistan: IRGC and Quds Force; A Recipe for Disaster?" National Council of Resistance of Iran. November 2007,14. http://www.ncr- iran.org/en/news/iran-world/-4363afghanistan-irgc-and-quds-force-a-recipe-for-disaster.

(81) Katzman, Kenneth, Iranian Revolutionary Guards, Op. cit. 27-26.

(82) See: The Seventh Day. July 2017,10.

(83) Nader, Alireza. "Iran After the Bomb, How Would a Nuclear-Armed Tehran Behave?" National Security Research Division, RAND. 25 .2013.

(84) Zahran, Yosra. "Revolutionary Guard, A Different Doctrine of Combat." Op. cit.

(85) Banerjea, Udit, "Revolutionary Intelligence." Op. cit. 102.

(86) "Iranian Revolutionary Guard in Details: 38 Years of Criminality and Terrorism." Orient Net. May 2017,2.

(87) al-Mansouri, Nour Uddin. "Iranian Minister Accuses the Revolutionary Guard of Smuggling Goods to the Country." The New Gulf. February 2017,4. http://www. thenewkhalij.org/ar/node/63713.

(88) "Rouhani Criticizes the Intervention of the Revolutionary Guard in the Iranian Economy." Gulf Online. April 2017,18.

(89) "Commander of the Revolutionary Guard Attacks Rouhani: We Have Rockets and Rifles." Middle East. June 2017,28.

(90) "Rouhani Criticizes the Intervention of the Revolutionary Guard in the Iranian Economy." Op. cit.

(91) "IRGC Commander Attacks Rouhani: We Own Missiles." Baghdad Post. June 2017,28. http://tbp.today/en/Story/36218.

(92) Nuruzzaman, Mohammad. "What Comes Next for Iran›s Defense Doctrine?" The National Interest. November 2016,10. http://nationalinterest.org/feature/what- comes- next- irans- defense- doctrine- 18360.

(93) "The IRGC: Saudi Arabia›s First Enemy." Al Arabiya.net. July 2016,21.

(94) See: Banerjea, Udit, "Revolutionary Intelligence." Op. cit. 105.

(95) See: Sadjadpour, Karim. Reading Khamenei: The World View of Iran's Most Powerful Leader. Carnegie Endowment for International Peace. 2009. http://carnegieendowment. org/files/sadjadpour_iran_final2.pdf.

(96) Wehrey, Frederic et al. Dangerous But Not Omnipotent. Op. cit. 39.

The Iranian Military Institution: Combat Capabilities, Deployment Plans, and Functions

Saad Mohammad Ibn Nami (Ph.D.)
Iranian Studies Researcher

Summary

This paper discusses the development of Iran's military institu- tion, analyzing its combat capabilities and its doctrinal change, as well as its traditional and strategic deployment plans to achieve military superiority and interfere in regional countries. To achieve its goals, Iran has exploited its sectarian proxy militias to expand its capability and influence, as well as submerging the region in conflict.

The Iranian Military Institution

During the reign of the Shah, Iran's military turned into a pow- erful institution in the Gulf. The Shah built a strong army to take control of the Gulf - especially after British withdrawal from the region. He believed Gulf security could be achieved through one of two ways; ensuring Iran's military power was stronger than the Gulf States' or persuading the Gulf States to enter a strong alliance with Iran. The Shah believed he was the protector of the West's interests, in particular of about 60% of the world's oil re- serves, which drove him to develop strong conventional and un- conventional military capabilities to take control of the Hormuz Strait and the International Shipping Lanes. In fact, Iran's strate- gic goal as a regional power was concentrated on finding a unique regional position among countries such as Iraq, the Kingdom of Saudi Arabia, Turkey, Egypt, and Israel, as well as maintaining a balance of power with countries with a nuclear programme like Pakistan and Israel.[1]

The Shah deployed his army outside and inside the country. For example, Iran's army was involved in designing the 1953 coup, in cooperation with the CIA, which resulted in the Shah being re- stored to power, and the appointment of a military government under the leadership of Major General Zahidi, the Command- er-in-Chief of the Iranian Army.[2]

The Shah relied on Iran's armed forces to face internal unrest in the country. For example, in 1963 tribal chiefs and clerics led the opposition against agrarian reforms,[3] but they were repressed by the army. However, with the growing tensions of the 1979 revo- lution, the army could not control the conditions and protect the Shah or dissuade him from leaving the country. This demoralized the army commanders at that time. To prevent clerics from taking over the country, army commanders tried to carry out a military coup in Iran, but they were frustrated by the United States when General Robert E. Huyser came to Tehran and convinced army commanders to stop their coup and to support Shahbour Bakh- tiar after the Shah's departure from the country.[4]

When the Islamic regime took over the country, Iran's army was strong and equipped with US state of the art arms. In the beginning, the army remained neutral, but Khomeini, eventually, prosecuted some army commanders and dismissed others, which squeezed Iran's military capability by causing a decline in their command staff and size. Also, the US and Europe halted the sale of arms and spare parts to Iran.[5] After the revolution, the Iranian military institution witnessed remarkable changes and was linked to the Supreme Leader, the Higher Commander of the Armed Forces, as stated in the Iranian constitution, which granted him considerable powers in appointing and dismissing military and security commanders. The Iranian constitution made the role of the armed forces clear in article 143, "The army of the Republic of Iran is responsible for defending the independence of the country and its territorial integrity." Also, in Article 151, "The government is obliged to provide a programme of military training, with all requisite facilities, for all its citizens, in accordance with Islamic criteria, in such a way that all citizens will always be able to en- gage in the armed defense of the Islamic Republic of Iran." Howev- er, it states, at the same time, that the possession of arms requires the granting of permission by competent authorities.[6]

The Iranian Military Doctrine

A military doctrine relates to a state's official military policy when it comes to military conflict, operations, and engagement, as well as how to prepare the country and its armed forces for war.[7]

Military Doctrine Characteristics:[8]

» A military doctrine is the formal expression of military knowl- edge the armed forces comply within war. It sets the key prin- ciples of leadership, tactics, training, support operations and managing equipment necessary for success and the continuity of military maneuvers.

» A military doctrine is developed at the highest level in a coun- try under supervision of the military leadership to achieve its military goals.

» A military doctrine is developed by carrying out scientific re- search and historical studies involving all the state's vital ac- tivities to design and define points of view in armed conflicts.

» A military doctrine is turned into rules, principles, and theo- ries which are taught to army commanders and personnel in the various military colleges, institutes, and schools. In addi- tion, army training is aligned with these rules and principles in peacetime, in the daily and annual military exercises, and ulti- mately, practically applied in war times.

» A military doctrine is the primary driver of the military forces, which means that the superiority of these forces on the ground is closely linked to the doctrine they have adopted. In fact, this doctrine is the driver of military forces, individually and col- lectively, to succeed under all conditions requiring resilience and sacrifice. The other factors of success, like experience and organization, come next in importance.

» A military doctrine of any country is based on the religion and values of that country. No country can adopt any doctrine that goes against its values and religion or order its army command- ers and military forces to train on such a doctrine violating its established principles.

Levels of military doctrine:[9]

» Fighting Doctrine
» Combat Doctrine
» Fighting Ideology

Types of military doctrine:[10]

» Basic doctrine: the basic principles to determine and guide the general framework of the military doctrine in any country.
» Environmental doctrine: the basic principles adopted by the major units of any country's armed forces.
» Organizational doctrine: the basic principles adopted by the various units of any military force to carry out their missions and accomplish their goals.

Sources of military doctrine:[11]

» The state's comprehensive doctrines such as ideology and the principles recognized by political leaders of any country
» Past experiences
» Technical development
» Sources of threat and evolution in the world order
» Nature of the next war
» The state's military strategy
» The state's geography
» Current and future functions

The military doctrine of Iran's army during the Shah's period (1943-1979) was similar to the US and European doctrines as it purchased its arms and equipment from these countries. The Shah regularly delegated army officers to visit these countries for training and to implement the updating of Iran's military doctrine to align it with Europe and the United States, as well as to develop Iran's military capability with it becoming the strongest marine, ground, and air force in the region at that time.

After the Iranian revolution, many military commanders with extensive military experience were exposed to trials, executions, and imprisonment, while others fled the country. The majority of those executed were Navy Commanders for being close to the Shah before his fall. This witch-hunt harmed Iran's army and its capability as it lost its most experienced commanders in military training and carrying out its military doctrine on the ground in wartime. To fill the vacuum in the regular armed forces and to restore the balance of power with these forces, the revolutionary regime gave life to the Iranian Revolutionary Guard Corps (IRGC). The IRGC was tasked with protecting the new regime internal- ly against any reaction by the Iranian regular army. In addition, when the Iraq-Iran war broke out, the new regime in Iran called for volunteers to join the IRGC to go to war, which resulted in a third armed entity, albeit one lacking training and organization. Under such conditions, the Iranian armed forces could not implement its military doctrine adequately, but adopted an old strategy relying on subsequent human waves in wartimes.[12]

Evolution of the Iranian Military Doctrine

Some researchers believe Iran adopted a defensive military doctrine post-1979 revolution to achieve two fundamental goals: to prevent enemies from attacking Iran, and; to achieve self-suf- ficiency in defense capabilities in all fields. This doctrine went through three stages:

Between the end of the first Gulf war until 2001: In this stage, the Iranian regime depended on local capability and the ability to inflict huge losses on enemy forces on the ground to prevent them from beginning any attacks on Iran.

Post-9/11 events: In this stage, the Iranian military doctrine shifted towards the development of missiles, an inclination to- wards having nuclear weapons, and unconventional warfare. The fall of Saddam Hussein and the US invasion of Iraq in 2003 gave ground for the Iranian regime to combine conventional warfare strategies of deterrence with psychological deterrence strate- gies and asymmetric warfare. In 2005, the Iranian armed forces - headed by the IRGC - reshaped its defense doctrine completely and called it the "Mosaic Defence" to face US troops stationed in Afghanistan and Iraq in case they decided to attack Iran. Basically, this new doctrine relied on mass mobilization and asymmetric warfare strategies.

Post-Arab Spring in 2011: This stage witnessed significant changes in the Iranian defense doctrine. Currently, Iran is engaged in battles outside its borders to fight ISIS in Iraq and to support Bashar Assad in Syria. This new doctrine increases Iran's influ- ence outside its borders and maintains its support to Shiite proxy militias in Iraq, Lebanon, Syria, Yemen, and other countries.[13]

Platform of the Iranian military doctrine[14]

- » State's religious ideology
- » The Iranian constitution
- » Foreign policy
- » Conspiracy theory and fears of regional and international threats.

Combat Capabilities of the Iranian Armed Forces Iran's military spending

The nuclear-related sanctions imposed on Iran by the inter- national community decreased the Iranian military spending by 30% from 2006-2015. In 2016, Iran's military budget amounted to $10 billion USD, as stated by the Stockholm International Peace Research Institute (SIPRI). However, this situation changed after signing the Iranian nuclear deal in 2015 between Iran and the P 5+1 group. The US and EU lifting of sanctions strengthened the Iranian economy and increased Iranian military spending. The Iranian members of parliament adopted the "Fifth Plan for Devel- opment," approved by the Iranian Supreme Leader, Ali Khamenei, in July 2015. It stated that the Iranian government would develop Iran's defense capabilities to be a regional power, and safeguard Iran's security and interests, by allocating 5% of its annual bud- get to the Iranian armed forces and there was an increase in the budget of the Iranian naval forces. In fact, this significant increase in Iranian military spending could be used for developing ballistic missiles, armed drones, and cyber capabilities.[15]

The Iranian military industry

Iran has made significant strides in this field compared to the Arab and Third World countries. The Military Industries Commis- sion in the Ministry of Defence, with the support of the Iranian armed forces, oversees military plants and industries in Iran.

Iran produces all its military equipment, including warplanes and tanks, but this industry has not reached advanced levels. It can be classified as out-of-date when compared to the state-of- the-art arms and equipment bought by the GCC countries from all over the world. In reality, the Iranian military industry is nothing but a re-engineering of old-fashioned arms such as the Thunder- bolt airplane, which is a carbon copy of the US F-5 warplane.[16]

Some reports have revealed that the Iranian military industry has gone through four stages:[17]

» The first stage preceded the Iraq-Iran war, and the sector wit- nessed a significant decline.

» The second stage started with the beginning of the Iraq-Iran war and concentrated on producing ammunition for the armed forces involved in war.

» The third stage followed the end of the Iraq-Iran war when many production lines were opened to manufacture arms and military equipment after the Ministry of Defense and Revolu- tionary Guards were combined, and the Army Defense Indus- trial Establishment was combined with the IRGC Self Sufficien- cy Establishment in 1990.

» The final stage started after September 11, when the Iranian military industries witnessed tremendous strides in all fields, including missiles.

The Iranian Military Capabilities Regular Army

The Iranian armed forces are estimated numbering around 523,000 soldiers; 340,000 in the Army, 125,000 IRGC elements, 18,000 Navy forces, and 40,000 mobilizing troops. In 2016, the Iranian government allocated 2.7% (15.9 billion USD) of its GNP for the Iranian armed forces.[18] According to the Iranian military structure, the Iranian ground, navy, and air defense forces report to the army, which is considered one of the strongest armies in the Middle East. Iran has developed a significant military indus- try, relying on its nucleus military industry established by the Shah by the end of his era. Some military experts believe the Ira- nian armed forces are amongst the strongest in the Middle East.[19] Global Firepower (GFP) released the Iran Military Strength report for 2017, which mentioned that the Iranian ground forces have about 1616 basic combat tanks, more than 1315 armored combat vehicles, 320 self-propelled artillery pieces, and more than 2398 artillery and missile pieces. The Iranian air force has 477 war- planes, 203 transport aircraft, 65 trainer aircraft, and 138 combat helicopters. The navy has 398 frigates, destroyers and boats, and 33 submarines. Statistically, Iran was ranked 21 out of 133 coun- tries considered for GFP review for the year 2017.[20]

Revolutionary Guards

The IRGC achieved superiority over the regular army, which had remained a source of threat to the 1979 revolution for a long period. The IRGC played a major role in stability by repressing Iran's enemies inside and outside the country. Constitutionally, the IRGC reports to the Supreme Leader, giving this institution great powers in the country. The constitution article 150 men- tions that the IRGC abides by the law, but this institution, which was founded as a revolutionary organization, has never observed the law or worked within its limits. On the contrary, it has tak- en control of all Iranian political, security, and social spheres. During the Iraq-Iran war, the IRGC became an influential force, as it turned from defending the revolution to defending the nation. When Iran was defeated in this war, the IRGC improved its role by turning into a force of resistance against Iraqi forces and achieved notable victories that gave it ground to take control of all Iranian internal affairs.[21] In the beginning, the IRGC was composed of a random mixture of local independent groups, city militants, mi- litias, deserters, and Khomeini hardliners. At that time, the IRGC did not have an official chain of command, and its commanders established their own individual roles and job descriptions. Later, the IRGC improved in structure and reorganized its units into le- gions, divisions, and brigades on the model of any regular army in the world. However, after the Iraq-Iran war, the IRGC made some amendments to its structure and function. In 1985, the IRGC formed air and naval units, and developed an official structural method to enlist and train soldiers who strove to promote the revolution all over the world by all means. The IRGC developed infrastructure for logistics and support for its forces, founded an independent Procurement Body, and built plants for military industries to circumvent the arms sanctions imposed on Iran by the international community. The IRGC's notable distinction was the constant improvement in its arms supply, which it claimed was manufactured locally under the supervision of the Ministry of the Revolutionary Guards, independent of the Ministry of De- fense. The IRGC established special units equipped with state-of- the-art arms - armoured vehicles, air defense systems, missiles, and others - which indicates the improvement and institutional complexity of this organization, knowing that the IRGC started fighting in the Iraq-Iran war using light weapons only.[22] There are different estimates of the number of IRGC elements. According to the International Institute for Strategic Studies in London, the IRGC is comprised of 350 thousand elements, while the Strategic and International Studies Institute states the number was only 120 thousand elements. The IRGC has significant combat capabil- ity, such as missiles that can send cluster warheads consisting of 1400 bomblets on target. The IRGC has made significant improve- ments to its military capability during recent decades - especially in its drone industry, missiles (including Shahab 1, 2, and 3), air defense, and electronic warfare systems. In addition to military activities, the IRGC is involved in many economic projects, worth billions of USD, in the oil, gas, and infrastructure fields. It has many large financial and investment institutions inside Iran involved in the production and services sectors such as constructions, roads, oil, and communication.[23] The total number of the Iranian armed forces amounted to more than 520,000 elements and 350,000 reserves. Some of the arms and equipment of these forces was purchased from the

United States and Europe before the Irani- an 1979 revolution. After that, the Iranian regime bought arms and military equipment from Russia, mainly, in the first months of the nineties during the last century. The Iranian armed forces have various models of the former Soviet Union and Russian arms including warplanes, helicopters, submarines that work on elec- tricity and diesel, tanks, armoured vehicles, air defense missile systems, and air missiles. In April 2016, Russia handed over the first shipment of the S-300 air defense missile systems to Iran.[24] The Iranian naval forces are great in number. They are equipped with submarines, frigates, warships, and fast boats while the GCC countries have more superior air capabilities in terms of the num- ber of warplanes, choppers, and ground to air missile launchers.[25]

Ballistic Missiles

Ballistic missile development is Iran's top priority. By the end of the last century, Iran had reached the same level as Iraq before the second Gulf War in 1991. Iran built a complete infrastructure, including 100 sites and 1,000 individuals prepared for working on this project, and sent about 5,000 individuals to receive mili- tary training in Russia, North Korea, China, the former Yugoslavia, Romania, India, and Brazil in 1992. For continuous development of this technology, Iran dealt with the world biggest arms compa- nies in Russia, China, and India, and built arms plants for the IRGC such as the Shaheed Hamat Industrial Group, the Fatih Factory, the Iranian Air Industries Development company, as well as other companies and plants.[26]

The following table includes the most important Iranian short, medium, and long-range ballistic missiles:[27]

Name	Range (in Kilometers)	Weight of the explosive warhead (in Kilogram)	Fuel type
Fajr-3	45	45	Solid
Fajr-5	75	75	Solid
Zilzal-1	150	600	Solid
Zilzal-2	200	600	Solid
Zilzal-3	250	-	-
Fatih-110	200-300	500	Solid
Shihab-1	350	1000	Liquid
Shihab-2	700	750	Liquid
Shihab-3	1330-2000	760	Liquid
Qiam	700-800	750	Liquid
Shihab-4	200-3000	1100	Liquid

Shihab-5	5000	1500-2000	Liquid
Qadir-1	1600	750	Liquid

Nuclear Program

Some observers believe the Iranian nuclear program was a heavy burden on the new regime, having been inherited from the Shah, while others believe the events following the Iraq-Iran war drove the new regime to revive its Iranian nuclear program. Nev- ertheless, Iran still sticks to its nuclear ambitions as a legitimate right to achieve the following goals:[28]

> » Make up for the shortfall in its conventional defense capabili- ties to play its regional role in the Arabian Gulf, which does not differ from the goal of the Shah before the 1979 revolution.
> » Iran has a dream of expanding its influence, building a great national state, and realizing its Shiite Crescent extending from Central Asia to the occupied territories in Palestine.
> » Nuclear weapons shall uphold Iran's attitude in case of any confrontation with the United States and its allies.
> » Maintain Iran's regional position to interfere in the internal af- fairs of the GCC countries.

Iran's ambition has raised concern in the world- especially the United States, Israel, and Iran's neighboring countries, knowing that the Iranian nuclear program might change Iran's military doctrine into an offensive and hostile one. Notably, there are no accurate statistics on Iranian military capabilities because of the lack of precise official information on the Iranian military budget; its arms deals with other countries and the size of its local arms production. In addition, Iran pays significant attention to uncon- ventional warfare such as Public Mobilization (Basij Forces), in- ternal security units, paramilitary units, and long-range ballistic missiles.[29]

Deployment Plans and Functions

This means to deploy or spread units, institutions, or activities in limited areas to stand against Iran's enemies.[30] Historically, the Iranian forces relied on the deployment of conventional forces in- cluding armored, mechanical, and infantry units stationed near the Iraqi and Turkish borders and equipped with conventional defense systems based on the expected approaches of the enemy, strategic sites, and vital geographic areas.[31] After the end of the Iraq-Iran war in 1988, Iran established a number of naval bas- es on its coastline with the Arabian

Gulf and the Gulf of Oman, and on the UAE islands. It updated its naval fleet, supplied it with new arms, and increased its combat capabilities by intensifying naval exercises.[32] In recent years, the Iranian navy has intensified its presence in international waters under directives of the Irani- an Supreme Leader, the Higher Commander of the armed forces, by deploying about eighty naval vessels in the Gulf of Aden and the strategic Strait of Bab Mandab. Some of these vessels have confronted naval piracy in the Gulf of Aden and escorted more than 3844 trade ships and oil tankers. They succeeded in liberat- ing some hostages and trade ships confiscated by Somali pirates in the Gulf of Aden, including a Chinese ship. Furthermore, the Iranian army naval forces plan to establish two maritime zones comprising three military bases on the Iranian coast in the Sea of Oman.[33]

IRGC navy is deployed in the following five naval zones:[34]

» Sahib Zaman in Bandar Abbas and is considered one of the most important IRGC zones.
» Prophet Noah in Bushehr
» Imam Hussein in the port of Mahshehr
» Tha'erullah in the Slawiyah economic zone which lies within the largest gas and oil reserves in the Middle East.
» Imam Mohammad Baqir in the port of Lanjah.
» This is one of the most important IRGC zones.

It extends from Qashm island to Kish island - the district includ- ing the occupied UAE islands Smaller Tunb, Greater Tunb, and Abu Mousa - in addition to Siri Island, 40 kilometers to the west of Abu Mousa island, as shown in the following map:[35]

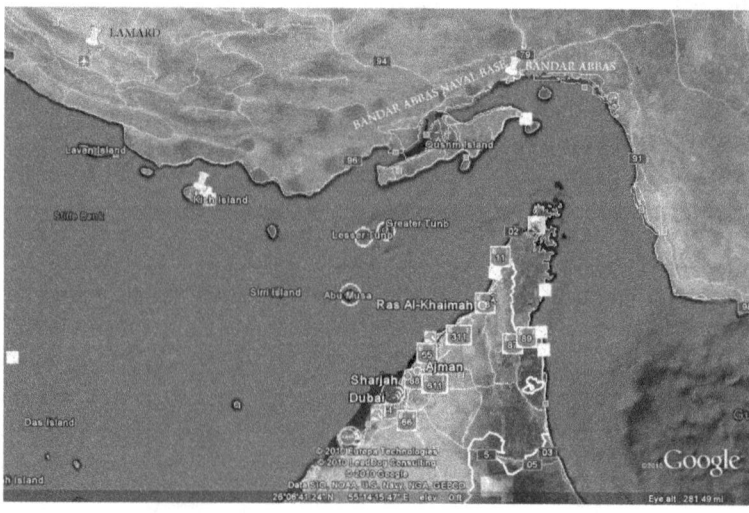

Iran has other naval bases in the Arabian Gulf including the Shaheed Mahlalti Naval Base, the Bushehr Naval Air station, the Arvand base for air surveillance at the mouth of Shat al-Arab, the Imam Ali Naval Base in Chabahar, Jask, the naval missile silo base, and other bases at the Tahiri port. Also, Iran has other naval facilities on the Karj, Farsi, Kashm, Lark, and Lavan islands. The IRGC has established an extended network of underground tunnels and missile silos on the Arabian Gulf Islands, which has turned these islands into "Fixed Warships."[36]

On the ground, the Syrian crisis is another example of Iran's interference in the affairs of other countries. The Iranian regime interfered in Syria by sending some IRGC advisors to this coun- try in 2012. Their participation was limited to training, assisting, and giving advice to Syrian senior army commanders. In Sep- tember 2015, this strategy changed, and the IRGC ground forces were deployed in Syria after Russian interference in this country. Throughout 2016, the Iranian regime increased its operations in Syria when it blockaded the city of Aleppo and took it back from the Syrian armed opposition. In this battle, the IRGC Quds legion participated side by side with the IRGC ground forces.[37] In addi- tion to the aforementioned strategies, Iran has adopted other un- conventional plans as follows:

A-Incursion

During the US invasion of Iraq in 2003, Iran adopted the strate- gy of constructive neutrality - the same posture it adopted as the US invaded Afghanistan. When the United States was preparing for the invasion of Iraq, some US officials believed in involving Iran in this operation, tactically, as a beginning for broader collab- oration between both sides. Accordingly, the two countries held a narrow path of negotiations on Iraq and its future, but a state of mistrust and uncertainty prevailed between them.[38] Through its neutral position, Iran sought to preserve its interests in Iraq by adopting a bilateral strategy; on the one hand, Iran support- ed the Iraqi opposition groups in contact with the United States. This support was not initiated by the Higher Council for Islamic Revolution in Iraq only, but also by the Iraqi National Summit, the Kurdish Democratic Party, and the National Union in Kurdistan to establish a democratic, inclusive government in Iraq. On the other hand, the IRGC and Iranian Intelligence broke into Iraq with thou- sands of Badr militants, who received training from the hands of the IRGC in Iran to carry out their assigned strategic plans after the fall of Saddam Hussein by supporting and strengthening Shi- ites waiting to benefit from the political changes resulting from a new Iraq. These militias found their way in due to the security vacuum resulting from the fall of the Iraqi security services fol- lowing the US invasion of Iraq.[39] Iran planted its seeds in Iraq; a strategy Iran has adopted in any territory inhabiting

Shiites, waiting for the day and appropriate circumstances to reap the benefits of its practices, which was revealed by the former late President Rafsanjani when he said that Iran helped Shiites - even a party or parliamentary minority - everywhere. To avoid clashes with the US troops in Iraq and future American threats, Iranian officials strove to establish a Shiite security cordon around Iran.[40] The absence of an Arab political and military strategy and region- al role paved the way for Iran to expand its influence, utilizing the US invasion of Iraq and the Shiite sect in the region;[41] otherwise, Iran could not have singled out Iraq, Yemen, Syria, Lebanon, and Palestine and become, through its agents, a major regional player at the expense of the Arab countries. Some Arab intellectuals be- lieve the absence of an Arab project has opened the door for Iran to expand its influence to preserve its interests in its vital sphere. However, others argue that the absence of an Arab project did not give Iran the right or legitimacy to violate the sovereignty of Arab countries, which means denying Iranian interference and expan- sionist ambitions and confronting its regional project.[42]

B-Proxy war

Iran provides constant support to its proxy militias in Iraq and Yemen and has dispatched sectarian militias to Syria to partic- ipate in the civil war in this country. The following are some of these militias:

Sectarian militias in Iraq:[43]

- » Badr Legion
- » Mahdi Army
- » Asa'ib Ahl Haq
- » Mukhtar Army
- » Abu Alfadhl Alabass Brigade

Sectarian militias in Syria:[44]

- » The Lebanese Hezbollah
- » Abu Fazl Abbas Brigade
- » Zulfiqar Brigade
- » The Iraqi Hezbollah Battalions
- » Sayyed Shuhada Battalions
- » Mohammad Baqir Sadr Forces (Badr Organization- the military wing)
- » Kafeel Zainab Brigade
- » Hezbollah Nujaba Movement
- » Wa'd Sadiq Legion
- » Assadullah Ghalib Brigade

» Imam Hussein Brigade
» Rapid Intervention Regiment
» Fatimiyoun and Zaynabioun Divisions

Sectarian militias in Yemen (Houthis). The Iranian Cyber Army

This army started as an electronic warfare battalion in the Ira- nian regular army. Then, the Iranian Supreme Leader gave orders to move the unit to be under the leadership of the IRGC because of serious electronic warfare and cyber attack threats targeting the Iranian nuclear and space programs.[45]

The following are the most important events that drove Iran to pay great and increasing attention to improve its cyber army:

» The 2009 Green Revolution
» The 2010 Stuxnet Virus
» The 2011 Stars and Duqu Viruses
» The Flame Virus
» The Iranian Cyber Army subgroups:[46]
» The Qassam Cyber Fighters Group (QCF)
» The Parasto Group
» The Syrian Cyber Army

The Iranian cyber army is deployed in several territories but the focus is on its presence in Iraq, for two reasons. The first is that Iraq shares borders with the Kingdom of Saudi Arabia, Ku- wait, and Jordan, while the second reason is that poverty and the backward way of life in South Iraq facilitated the enlisting of Iraqi sectarian youth, who work in cheap rooms in houses or distant locations for low wages and administer hundreds of social media accounts by conducting discussions and sectarian incitement.[47]

Recommendations

Iran has significant military and electronic warfare capabili- ties, which oblige the Arab world to take countermeasures to face Iranian ambitions. Regionally, the GCC countries need a strategic project to face Iran's plans, based on political, social, and military aspects. This project must be part of a greater Arab strategy to drive Iran out of Arab countries it has controlled, destabilized, and seized. Indeed, now is an opportune moment with the com- mencement of the Saudi-led Decisive Storm operation, which has frustrated Iranian plans of controlling Yemen and threatening the security of the Kingdom of Saudi Arabia, as part of a comprehen- sive plan targeting the whole region. In addition, the Arab media and intellectual sectors must take on the challenge of preventing

Iran from spreading its sectarian tendencies and promoting the Shiite sect in the region. They must face the Iranian media, in par- ticular, its lies, propaganda, and programs targeting the Arab and Gulf social fabric. There must be a focus on teaching Farsi, and the work of the Farsi Departments in Saudi universities must focus on both the media and intellectual sectors. On the intelligence and military levels, Arab and regional countries must intensify their efforts in discovering Iranian spying networks. These networks try to gather information on all the regional countries by recruit- ing spies in these countries to conspire against their homelands and harm their social and security stability. Militarily, Arab and regional countries must build advanced military technologies and arms to achieve superiority over Iran - the GCC countries in par- ticular and Arab World in general. These countries must conduct joint military exercises and improve the readiness of their forces. Moreover, the Saudi-led Arab coalition has to take control of the international waters in the area extending from the Sea of Oman through the Hormuz Strait up to the Bab Mandeb Strait to prevent Iran from smuggling arms to the Houthi rebels in Yemen and to other countries.

Endnotes

(1) Issam, Naiel Almajali. The Impact of the Iranian Armament on the Gulf Security, Amman, Hamid Library for Publishing and Distribution, 1ˢᵗ edition: 2012, p68-67.

(2) Dr. Hamid, Ahmad (translated). Custody Secrets, CIA Confidential Documents Concerning the Overthrowing of Dr. Mosaddegh, translated by Dr. Hamid Ahmad, Tehran: Nashr-e-Nari, 1ˢᵗ Edition, 2000, p. 32-30.

(3) Antony, Paisons. Diaries of the last British Ambassador in Iran during the Shah era. Translated by: Doctor Khalid Saleem, Ahmad, Beirut: Arabian Publishers for Encyclopedia, 1ˢᵗ edition, 2010, p95.

(4) Ibid, p163.

(5) Issam, Naiel Almajali. The Impact of the Iranian Armament on the Gulf Security, previous reference, p79.

(6) The Iranian constitution released in 1979 including amendments up to 1989, translated by the International Institution for Democracy and Elections, updating the project of comparative constitutions, "constituteproject.org", December 2014,15, p27.

(7) Major General Pilot Abdurrahman Hassan Ashahri: Evolution of Military Doctrines and Strategies, Riyadh, Obeikan Library, 1ˢᵗ edition 2003, p65.

(8) Dr. Khaled Ibn Abdullah Addibian. Ibn Tomart, founder of the Unitarian State Military Doctrine. http://soo.gd/ZXF5

(9) Ibid, p. 63.

(10) Ibid, p73-68.

(11) Military Doctrine, April 2017,5, http://cutt.us/isAMI

(12) Fighter from Desert Encyclopedia website, the Iraqi-Iranian war from the Arab point of view, chapter 11 (Lessons Learned from Applied Combat doctrines). http://cutt.us/ n2uXj

(13) National Interest: the upcoming change in the Iranian Military doctrine is suspicious. http://cutt.us/H7yEE

(14) The site of the Holy Defense News Agency, explaining the role and place of the airwaves in the military doctrine of the Islamic Republic of Iran, 2017/4/11, http://cutt. us/xp1gQ

(15) Moyen-Orient, Importante hausse annoncée des dépenses militaires iraniennes, http://cutt.us/li2wz, 2017-01-10

(16) Hassan, Fathi Qishaw. The Iranian Military Force... Delusion of the Present and Reality of the Future, Opinions on the Gulf Journal website, July 2017,15. http://soo.gd/ ftAd

(17) Haider, Razavi. The Iranian Military Capabilities in the Gulf, Tours website. http:// soo.gd/yRsF

(18) The Military Balance 2017. The International Institute for Strategic Studies, 2017/12/15. http://soo.gd/Ptbf http://soo.gd/Lsu2

(19) The Iranian Political System, Syria Center for Researches and Studies, January,27 2014. http://soo.gd/1Sht

(20) 2017 Iran Military Strength, (www.globalfirepower.com): http://soo.gd/ nuUT

(21) Ahmad, Katib. His orders: from the Government or Intelligence? IRGC Khameneiꞌs last card, Katib website. http://soo.gd/JeTP

(22) Kenneth Katzman. The IRGC, translated and printed by the Emirates Center for Strategic Studies and Researches, 1st edition, 1996, p24-23.

(23) Aljazeera. The IRGC. http://soo.gd/yMqX

(24) RT Arabic website: What is the size of the Iranian military force? June 2006,13. http://soo.gd/7TAh

(25) Dr. Taj Uddin, Ja'far Ta'i. The Iranian strategy toward the GCC countries, Damascus: Raslan Establishment for printing, publishing, and distribution, Ed. 1, p. 206-200.

(26) Isam, Naiel Almajali. The impact of the Iranian armament on the Gulf security, previous reference, p71-70.

(27) Retired Staff Brigadier General, Nizar, Abdulqadir. The Iranian missile program; its development and impact on the regional balance of power, the Lebanese National Defense Journal, issue 97, July 2016. http://soo.gd/ r1oC

(28) Dr. Saad, Ibn Nami. The Iranian nuclear file between the US sanctions and Israeli threats, Middle Eastern Studies Journal, issue 59, the Middle East Studies Center, Jordan, p87.

(29) Mustafa, Shafiq Allam. The State of Iran, determinants of strength and points of weakness, Cairo: the Arabian Center for Humanitarian Studies, international series, 2nd issue, December 2010, p64-63.

(30) Brigadier Sami Awad. Dictionary of Military Glossary, Amman, Osama Publishers, 1st edition, 2007, p. 65.

(31) Retired Staff Brigadier, Husam Sweilim: strategic analysis of the Iranian military force, Bawabah News, July 2017,20. http://soo.gd/ncEY

(32) Dr. Taj Uddin, Ja'far Ta'i. The Iranian strategy toward the GCC countries, Damascus.

(33) Hossein, Delirian. The Brilliant Future of the Iranian Navy, Re'ati. http://soo.gd/lvX6

(34) How can the Navy of the Revolutionary Guards be able to halt the Gulf and the Strait of Hormuz for the United States? At the time of Tabnak Ali. http://soo.gd/pR5D

(35) Where is the naval base of the Guards in the Gulf ?, the newspaper's website, http://soo.gd/ZOdn

(36) Retired Major General, Husam Sweilim. Iran's plan to humiliate the US fifth fleet in the Gulf, Arabian Gulf Center for Researchers and Studies. http://soo.gd/HDQp

(37) Paul, Bucala. Iran's New Way of War in Syria, Institute for the Study of War, February 2017/4/10,2017, http://cutt.us/W2XYE

(38) Flint, Levirate. The US-Iran relations: a look back… and the Imam View, previous reference, p13.

(39) Ibid, p. 14-13.

(40) Dr. Mohammad, Sa'eed Abdul Momin. Iran during President Khatami era. Modern civilizations studies center in the faculty of arts in the University of Ain Shams, Cairo, p58.

(41) Mohammad, Ahmad Muqdad. the impact of the Iranian internal and external changes on Iran's regional tendencies and Arab-Iran relations, case study, Studies Journal: Human and Social Sciences, part 40, Scientific Research Faculty, University of Jordan, p 461.

(42) Hassan, Shaheen. The Iranian expansion and absence of the Arab project, Arabi Jadeed newspaper, March 2015,4. http://soo.gd/qyfP

(43) Aljazeera net: the most prominent Shiite armed militias in Iraq. http://soo.gd/d2Jp

(44) Amir, Obaidah. A comprehensive file on the Shiite militias fighting in Syria, Noon Post website, January 2016,10. http://soo.gd/6fu4

(45) Dr. Nabil, Otoum. Iran's Cyber Army, Omayah Center for strategic researches and studies, Ammar for publishing and distribution. Electronic book, p. 23. http://soo.gd/ qbiQ

(46) Ali Hussein, Bakir. Iran's Cyber Army, Almajalah Journal, October 1:35,2013,27. http://soo.gd/ZILq

(47) Husam, Ta'i. Iran's Cyber Army, Alaraby Aljadeed website, February 2016,29. http:// soo.gd/m3jD

Militarization of Shiism

Mohammed Saqr Alsulami (Ph.D.)
Chairman of the International Institute for Iranian Studies (Rasanah)

Once the Iranian Revolution broke out, Khomeini – and his companions – paved a new path for Shiites inside and outside Iran as a guiding compass for the implementation of the "supreme Iranian strategy." They used different tools, under a doctrinal Shi- ite umbrella, to serve the sectarian Shiite project. At home, they eliminated their allies, who, according to Khomeini, had become a threat to the theory of *velayat-e faqih* (the Supreme Jurist Leader- ship). Abroad, they incited the Shiite communities to implement Iran's transboundary project in the countries of the so-called Shi- ite Crescent: Syria, Iraq, Yemen, Lebanon, and parts of the Arabian Gulf states.

Going forward with their project, the Iranian decision-makers ran the ideology of *velayat-e faqih* by creating new ideologized and militarized proxies that have the upper hand over the mil- itary institutions in post-revolutionary Iran. These military in- stitutions are marked by doctrinal tags that motivate fighters to defend them by their "doctrine" and not for their own interests. Had the communities politicized, they would have been milita- rized, according to the Iranian strategy, against the Sunni ruling regimes or to support the Shiite regimes. Iran's military institu- tions do not consider the consequences that would arise in the countries targeted by the Iranian expansionist project. The nation state may collapse because of sectarian conflicts, the spread of terrorism, separatist tendencies, and unorganized displacement of people. This study aims to theoretically evolve the concept of "militarizing Shiism." It applies this theory to Iranian domestic affairs and to the Arab countries where Iran has sought to milita- rize, arm, and mobilize the Shiite enclaves so that they stand as an impenetrable barrier in their own home countries, providing the ability to implement Iranian projects. The study also explores in depth the mutual interaction between "militarization" and "Shi- ism," clarifying the phenomenon of "militarizing Shiism" at home and abroad as the Iranians violate another state's sovereignty by interfering in its domestic affairs and supporting terrorist groups, thereby leading to a collapsing state.

First: Theoretical Framework

Definition of Shiism and militarization

Militarization is a term used in military science and weapon- ization. It is a noun derived from the verb "militarize," which Me- riam-Webster Dictionary defines as, "to give military character, to equip with military forces and defenses, to adapt for military use."[1]

Militarizing a group is the process of recruiting, arming, and teaching a group of people distinctive martial arts so that they become a powerfully armed entity ready to engage in wars and conflicts against the ruling regime or a minority sect of a diver- gent ideology. This policy – one country militarizing population groups outside its border so that it can implement its schemes and strategies – is seen in most developing countries in the world.[2]

*Shi'ism** means the world's Shiite communities, mostly (70- 80%) in four countries: Iran, Pakistan, India, and Iraq.[3] The *Factbook* page of the Central Intelligence Agen- cy (CIA) indicates that the total Muslim population in Iran is approximately 90% Shiites and 10% Sunnis.[4] However, several international and Arab media outlets have stated that the Shiite population in Iran is around 70%-81%.[5] Also, the *Factbook* page of the CIA stated that the total Iranian pop- ulation in 2017 was estimated at around 82 million inhabitants.[6] The total Shiite population in Pakistan, India, and Iraq is about 90 million; thus, Iran contains the highest percentage of the Shiite population in the world and the Middle East.

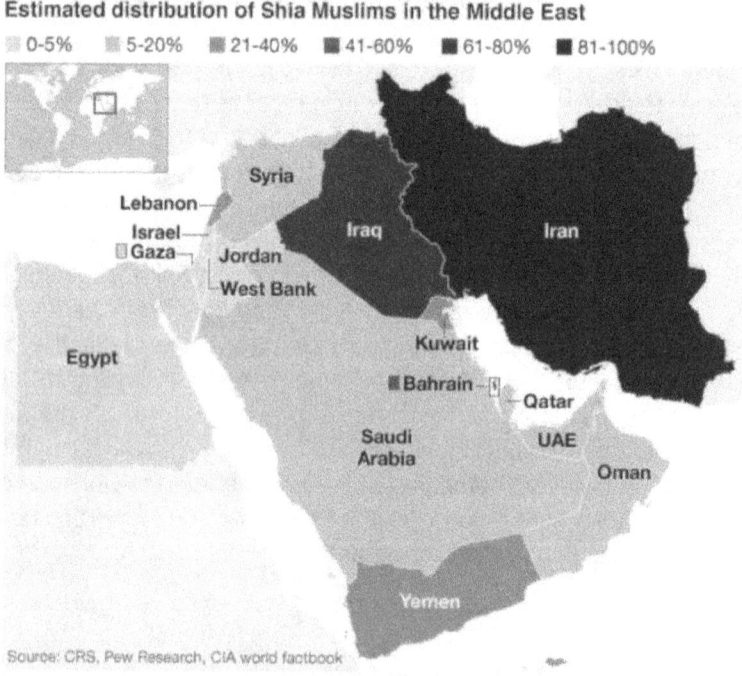

Source: http://cutt.us/3VASk

The largest of the Shiite groups is the Twelvers, followed by the Ismailis, then the Zaydis, the smallest of three Shiite subsects. Most Twelver Shiites live in Iran, Iraq, Azerbaijan, and Bahrain. A few of them live in Kuwait, Lebanon, some Saudi cities (Qatif, Al Ahsa, and Medina), Oman (Muscat and Batinah), Pakistan, India, and Central Asia. The Ismailis live in Najran (a city in Saudi Ara- bia) and India. Most of the Zaydi Shiites live in Yemen.

The number of Shiites in the world is estimated at around 150- 200 million, accounting for 10-13% of the world's Muslim popu- lation. Three-quarters of them (approximately 116-147 million) live in Asia, while one-quarter (35-44 million) live in North Africa.[7]

Concept of militarizing Shiism

Theoretically speaking, with militarizing and Shiism being linked, a simple definition of the term *militarizing Shiism* be- comes more evident based on dependent and independent vari- ables, where mutual interaction will eventually lead to militariz- ing Shiism.

First case: Militarizing is the independent variable while Shiism is the dependent variable

This case arises when an entity or statehood with a Shiite majority arms and trains its members on asymmetric warfare and guerrilla warfare tactics and recruits military and non-mil- itary fighters from politically and security-unstable states. These fighters become armed militias able to place pressure, spread influence, and forcefully execute agendas in their home countries. As a result, these countries will gradually become fragile and ready for occupation by the militarizing power.[8]

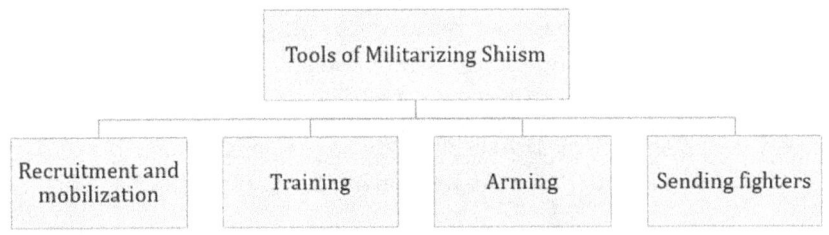

Second case: Shiism is the independent variable while militarizing is the dependent variable

This case arises when one entity or statehood infuses under- tones of Shiism in all branches of its military institutions to grant them a doctrinal symbolism and religious sacredness. When the two cases merge, the concept of *militarizing Shiism* becomes com- plete.

Practically speaking, in this study statehood reflects the theo- cratic republic of Iran since the 1979 revolution: the beginning of a new stage in Iran's international, regional, and domestic poli- cies. The 1979 revolution was the stepping stone of the Supreme Jurist Leader Khomeini and his companions in their efforts to mil- itarize Shiite groups at home and abroad.

The previously discussed concept of militarizing Shiism un- veils the mutual influence between *militarizing* and *Shiism* in the case of Iran. It starts with the influence of Shiite doctrine (Shiism) on the military institution and its mission inside Iran since the 1979 revolution, i.e., *the Shiite coloring prevails over-militarization*. Second, the military institution influences Shiism abroad, or in Iran's vital areas, i.e., the military coloring prevails over Shiism. Here, we have two variables or two tracks of mutual influence for applying militarizing and *Shiism* in Iran.

Mutual influence between militarizing and Shiism

Inside Iran

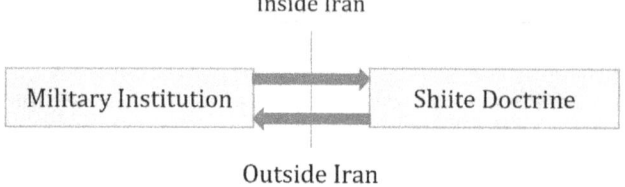

Outside Iran

First track: Shiism and militarizing

As previously discussed, this is based on coloring the entire military institution inside Iran and all its branches – military fighters, brigades, training camps, land-sea-air weapons, military colleges, military bases – with Shiism. This grants the military institution Shiism symbolism and doctrinal significance for its members through the use of several tools:[9]

> » Giving Shiite names to weapons, training camps, and military exercises;
> » Delivering Friday speeches at training camps of military fight- ers;

Sending clerics and *maddahis** to battlefields in the targeted countries;

> » Appointing clerics in military institutions and training camps;
> » Using religious slogans in military institutions and garrisons; and
> » Selecting representatives of Khamenei from among IRGC, in- cluding its corps and training camps.

This policy makes military and non-military fighters loyal to the Supreme Leader, and submissive and committed to his or- ders and teachings. They defend his theories and projects. In- side Iran, the practices of elimination and hazing are employed against those who adhere to sects other than Shia, such as the Arabs in Ahvaz, the Baluchis, and the Kurds. They are deprived of their fundamental rights and political freedoms and face death by hanging in public. Outside Iran, implementation of Iranian ex- pansionist projects is carried out by all means and ways in the targeted countries.[10]

Second track: Militarizing and Shiism

This is based on coloring Shiism (Shiite groups abroad) with military aspects through recruiting, training, arming, and sending fighters from unstable countries – such as Afghanistan, Pakistan, and Iraq – to fight in countries other than their own homelands. Shiite groups abroad are the armed proxies and enclaves in Iran's most vital and strategic areas used to fight for the Iranian project. Iran's strategically targeted areas are: [11]

» The Shiite Crescent: Iraq, Syria, Lebanon, Yemen, and parts of the Arabian Gulf are considered the most significant Iranian targets because they are geographically close to Iran, where a significant number of Shiites live who can implement Iran's project in these targeted countries. Arab-Iran relations cannot be assessed out of their historical background. The Arabs de- feated the Sasanian Empire (224- 651), the last Iranian empire before the adoption of Islam.[12] The Iranians believe that they are the first empire to spread its dominance into the Mediter- ranean Sea during the Achaemenid era. They returned to their status during the era of the Republic of Iran, according to the statement of the Second-in-Command, Hussein Salami.[13]

» Caucasia, Central Asia, Northwestern Asia, and the Caucasian Sea: These regions are fortresses against the historical Rus- sian ambitions, encompassing significant economic revenues. However, Iran did not consider this region to be a top priority because it is in the Russian sphere of influence. Russia has re- cently become Iran's regional ally, especially in the Syrian cri- sis. Therefore, the execution of Iran's project in this area shall be postponed until the path is smoothed out.[14]

» Geographically far regions: Africa, Latin America, Western Eu- rope, and the United States of America are the regions where Shiites exploit freedom of speech and democracy to create lob- bies which help maintain Iran's expansionist project by lever- aging decision-makers.

According to the consecutive order, militarizing Shiism occurs in the third stage of Iranian expansionism, preceded by two major stages. First is soft Shiism (spreading the Twelver Shiite doctrine using soft power tools such as establishing centers, holding con- ferences for rapprochement between Islamic sects, establishing charities, launching scholarship programs, the movie industry, inaugurating satellite channels, etc.). Second, politicizing Shiism is done by politicizing the Shiite enclaves and forging political movements – ideologically divergent from the ruling systems – under Iran's direct supervision. These movements reach a stage in which they believe that Iran is their homeland while they su- perficially belong to their true homelands, which they invade and plot against for the sake of the Iranian agenda.[15]

The fourth stage involves merging Shiism with the ruling sys- tems (to legitimize the presence of Shiite militias at home and abroad). The decision-makers have been using these tools since the 1979 revolution, taking into consideration the timing and the geopolitical conditions of the three regions. The stages are acti- vated consecutively in the targeted countries:

Shiism ⟶ politicizing ⟶ militarizing ⟶ merging In this study, we tackle the third stage: militarizing.

Second: The controversy of militarizing Shiism inside and outside Iran

Impact of Shiism on the IRGC

Once the Iranian revolution succeeded, the theocrats, the Su- preme Leader, and his companions directly created a power- ful military apparatus, one that surpassed the National Army in armaments and advanced military technology. It was the emer- gence of the IRGC with all of its corps: the Quds Force, the Basij, the Aerospace Force of the Army of the Guardians of the Islamic Revolution (AFAGIR) and the Navy of the Army of the Guardians of the Islamic Revolution (NEDSA).[16]

The Iranian regime started coloring the IRGC with Shiism by giving Shiite names to its branches, forces, and colleges. Also, the regime created an atmosphere of doctrinal support for and loyalty to Shiism among the Iranian military and citizens. Their goal was to forge a strong public grassroots effort that would give the decision-makers a "trump card" to spread their influence and boost the legitimacy of the Iranian regime, so that it could stand up against any regional or international claims. This clarifies the adhesive cohesion between Shiism and the IRGC personnel, who forcefully defend the IRGC's adopted decisions and policies at home or abroad.[17]

The Shiite IRGC bases and its brigades, manifested in sectarian undertones, are deployed across Iran: Tehran, Qom, Kermanshah, Hamedān, Elam, Khuzestan, Bushehr, Kerman, Sistan and Balu- chistan province, Isfahan, and Khorasan. Some of the most prom- inent Shiite names are- the base of Samen-ol-A'emeh and the base of *Ghadir, Valiasr's* brigade, *Tha'r Allah's* brigade [Revenge of God], Ashura's corps, and many other ideologized and sectari- anized names.[18] The Iranian regime gives Shiite names to its prox- ies abroad, such as *Fatimiyoun* from Afghanistan and *Zaynabioun* from Pakistan. Both of them fight in Syria under the Quds Force command on the pretext of defending Shiite holy sites.[19] The units and formations with doctrinal undertones are illustrated in table 1:

1.   Bases of doctrinal undertones:

The Shiite name of the base	Region	The Shiite name of the base	Region	The Shiite name of the base	Region
Hamza Chief of the Mar- tyrs	North- west of Iran	Karbala	North- east of Iran	Najaf Ashraf Base	Central region of Iran
Karbala	South- west of Iran	Samen-ol-A'emeh	South- east of Iran	Ghadir	North of Iran

2.   Brigades and battalions of doctrinal undertones

The brigade's Shiite name	Gover-nance/ City	The brigade's Shiite name	Gover-nance/ City	The battal-ion's Shiite name	Gover-nance/ City
27 Mech-anized Brigade Mohammad Rasol Allah	Tehran	43 Tha'r Al- lah' Brigade	Kar- man	44 Qa-mar bani Hashim Battalion	Shahr-e Kord
7th Ar-mored Brigade of Valiasr	Ahvaz	40 Sahib Alzaman Brigade	In a num-ber of gover-nances	12 Qa'im Battalion	Semnan
Imam Has-san Brigade	Isfahan	26 Ansar Almo'eme-neen	In a num-ber of gover-nances	82 Saheb ol Amr Bat- talion	Qazvin

3. Formations of doctrinal undertones:

The corps' Shiite name	Gover- nance/ City	The corps' Shiite name	Gover- nance/ City	The corps' Shiite name	Gover- nance/ City
Ashura Corps	Eastern Azerbaijan	Beit- ol-Mo- qaddas Corps	Kurdis- tan	Salman Corps	Sistan and Baluch- estan
Sahib Alzaman Corps	Isfahan	Imam Sajjad Corps	Hor- mozgan		
Valiasr Corps	Khuzestan	Ali bin Abi Talib Corps	Qom		

4. Colleges of doctrinal undertone

College	Governance/ City	College	Governance/ City
Imam Ali College (Army)	Tehran	Khatam al-An- bia Air Defense University	Tehran
Imam Hussein College (IRGC)	South-west of Iran	Imam Baqir University	Tehran

Data sources: Experts in Iranian affairs, Critical Threats Organization, https://bit. ly/2r0XGNp, CISIS, https://bit.ly/2HYS2Fg

Among the most doctrinal-marked military exercises Iran has carried out annually were:

» The *Velayat-96* naval drills for asymmetric wars, conducted on June 31, 2017, to provide military training in combat opera- tions for students of the Command and Staff College.

» The *Muḥarram* military drills conducted in August 2011, termed *"Ya Hussein,"* in coordination with *Khatam Anbia*, com- manded by the Deputy Commander of the IRGC (Hussein Sala- mi), and the commander of the IRGC Ground Force (Moham- mad Pakpour). It was held in Northwest Iran in coordination with the Hamza Chief of Martyrs, and it included an infantry unit, armored vehicles, forest combat, and missile and air de- fense systems.

» The *Heidar-e-Karrar* drill (*Heidar* is another name for Imam Ali), held in August 2017 in the South of Iran; various military units were involved, including the Rapid Reaction Unit, the Ar- tillery Unit, and the Drone Unit. [20]

Iran has never been confined merely to giving Shiite names to military units; the Iranian regimehas used many othertools, such as sendingclericsandFridayimamstothebattlefieldsinSyriaandIraq.[21] For example, Iranian media outlets reported that the Friday Imam of the Iranian city, Amol Jalil Mortazavi, was killed in one of the battles in Syria, where he was among the fighters. In addition, the Iranian regime appoints clerics in the military institutions and training camps to doctrinally motivate fighters and encour- age them to effectively and perfectly execute Iran's projects.

Moreover, the Iranian *maddahis* constitute one of the most sig- nificant Iranian tools in coloring the military with Shiism at home and abroad. An Iranian researcher of religious affairs, Mohammad Javad Akbarin, residing in France, told *Reuters* that the *maddahis* are of great significance to the Supreme Leader, as they can influ- ence and boost faith and belief among the fighters and citizens in regard to the Iranian project, whether inside or outside Iran.[22] They chant songs that motivate the fighters who are sta- tioned at the frontlines. The most prominent Irani- an *maddahis* are Hamid Reza Elemi and Saeed Hadaidan.[23] Akbarin said that the senior *maddahis* are bonded to the IRGC, the strongest military and economic power in Iran. Governmental institutions pay their salaries and assurance bills and give them loans. "The maddah, specifically, chant specialized songs ham- mering the importance of defending the holy sites such as the shrine of Sayyida Zainab near Damascus, which is considered one of the holiest Shiite sites," he said.

» An Iranian expert in IRGC issues, Ali Alfona, said the *madd- ahis* receive logistic support from the IRGC and the Leba- nese Hezbollah. Usually, they sing in the funeral lamenta- tions of the Iranian volunteers engaged in battles. While visiting a Syrian front, Hadadian was photographed wear- ing a camouflage patterned shirt and ammunition straps.

He said, "I went to Syria to show respect and appreciation to the fighters. They do what we cannot do but by words."[24] We cannot neglect to mention that the Supreme Leader has the right to appoint and depose senior leaders of the Nation- al Army and IRGC, such as the commander and deputy of the IRGC, the commanders of the Ground, Air, and Aerospace Forces, the commander of the Basij, the commander of the

Quds Force, the deputy of the Supreme Leader in the IRGC, and the assistant to the IRGC commander for coordination.[25]

The IRGC is directly affiliated with the Supreme Leader and not with any other governmental institutions, including the presiden- cy. It emerged from the heart of the revolutionary theocratic elite and is adhesively loyal to the Supreme Leader. Hojatoleslam Ali Saidi, the representative of the Guide for IRGC, coordinates be- tween the IRGC and the Supreme Leader and implements the pol- icies of the IRGC and the Supreme Leader at home and abroad.[26]

Impact of militarizing on Shiism (military proxies)

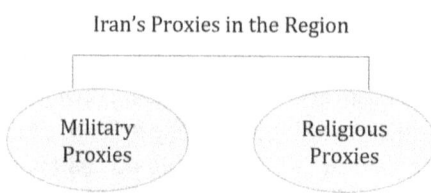

This variable explores the impact of militarizing the Shiite communities within the three strate- gically targeted areas to create armed and reli- gious proxies through recruiting, arming, and providing military training to those Shiite groups. The military training includes the use of a variety of weapons and combat fighting tactics required on the battlefields where Shiite groups will fight – in their home countries but in service to the Iranian expansionist and cross-boundary project. The variant military units, along with the military and paramilitary fighters, are sent to support the Shiite groups, enabling them to reach – by force – the ruling power in their home countries. At a minimum, they will help the Shiite groups destabilize and fragment their own home countries, smoothing the path toward occupation once they are unable to face the Shiite *armed* groups.[27]

This study specifically unveils militarizing Shiite communi- ties in the Shiite Crescent: Syria, Iraq, Yemen, Lebanon, and parts of the Arabian Gulf region. The sectarian texture of this region is marked by a considerable number of Shiites, who follow Shi- ite-Iranian Marja'. This region is geographically closest to Iran and has been suffering endless political and military conflicts since the breakout of the so-called Arab Spring in 2011. Therefore, this region is a priority for the Iranian expansionist project. Among the most significant indications of the militarization of the four countries – Syria, Iraq, Yemen, and Lebanon – though there are other regions facing militarization of Shiism:

1. Mobilization and recruitment

Mobilization and recruitment is the process of attracting peo- ple from the most unstable countries and sending them to fight in regional conflicts in the targeted countries, with the goal of executing the agenda of the recruiting power, whether it was a transnational organization or a country. The recruited fighters are promised both material and moral rewards – new national- ities and better living conditions than in their home countries.[28]

Following this perspective, the Mullah regime (the Supreme Jurist leader) since 1979 has been waiting for the right moment to pass its expansionist policies through the mobilization and recruitment of fighters abroad. Once the Iraqi regime was oust- ed, and the former Iraqi President Saddam Hussein was toppled in 2003, Khameini and his companions started recruiting Shiite fighters from unstable countries – like the *Fatimiyoun* brigade from Afghanistan, the *Zaynabioun* brigade from Pakistan, and the *Haidarioun* brigade from Iraq – to fight outside their home countries, especially in Syria and Iraq. In this regard, the Mullah regime had two major targets: Attack the Arab countries at home and get other countries involved in regional conflicts by recruit- ing their citizens in the regime's expansionist project.[29]

On December 10, 2017, the second-in-command of the IRGC, Hossein Salami, confessed that Iran had recruited fighters from Afghanistan, Pakistan, India, Lebanon, Iraq, and Iran. These indi- viduals were distributed among militias to fight in Syria under the pretext of battling the Americans and their allies. This is clear evidence of the Mullah regime's targets. The Iranian Tansim News Agency reported that Iran sent 30,000 fighters from the IRGC, the Lebanese Hezbollah, the Iraqi Shiite militias, and the Afghani Shi- ite militias to cover the severe shortage in the Syrian Army result- ing from increased defections after the Syrian crisis broke out.[30]

2. Training and preparing for warfare

This is the second stage after mobilization and recruitment. The fighters receive military training in the use of various weap- ons so that they become competent in guerrilla warfare and in implementing the recruiter's agendas.

The Quds of the IRGC, commanded by Major General Qasem Soleimani, is assigned to train the recruited fighters in the smug- gling of weapons and explosives, the targeting of security forces, the use and manufacture of weapons and high explosives, guerril- la warfare, the launching of missiles and terrorist attacks, hostage taking, assassinations, and the storming of Arab and Gulf embas- sies. Iran has approximately 14 military training camps inside it (see table 2: Iran's most significant training camps). The training camps are used to train fighters for the ongoing conflicts in Syria, Iraq, and Yemen. The fighters assist the militias in their military missions, with the goal being to spread their influence, by force, thereby boosting the cross-boundary Iranian expansionist proj- ect.[31]

Camp	Type of training	Camp	Type of training
Table 2: Iran's Most Significant Training Camps			
Imam Ali Academy	Theatrical train- ing	Lowshan Garrison	Training for spe- cial operations
Badindeh Center	For cities and suburbs	Chamran Garrison	Training Afghani elements and sending them to Syria
Amol (Malek Ashtar) Garrison	Coping with extremely harsh conditions	Aerial Center	Training commando forces
Samnan Garrison	Launching missiles	Abadan Garrison	Naval diving
Mashhad Garrison	Training Afghani elements	Gheshm Island Garrison	Urban guerrilla warfare
Pazouki Garrison	Training Afghani elements to fight in Syria	Center of "Mursad" Shiraz	Training foreign fighters

Data sources: Fox News, http://cutt.us/AzH63, Alarabiya, http://cutt.us/Zvb1R

Outside Iran, the IRGC established training camps distributed from Homs to Baalbek, North of Lebanon, stretching to Eritrea in Africa. Eritrea is geographically close to Yemen, which opens the gate for the IRGC to launch broader terror attacks. The IRGC es- tablished garrisons in Assab Port and the Dahlak Archipelago in the Red Sea. It has never stopped mobilizing and training young men for recruitment as fighters for Iran. The IRGC garrisons have reached the Guajira Peninsula, an isolated island located in the Caribbean between Northern Colombia and Northwestern Ven- ezuela.

In March 2015, the Italian Aki News Agency revealed that there are Iranian garrisons in Bosra and Izra' in the Dara`a governorate in Syria, where Houthi fighters receive military training in combat tactics in areas of conflict in Southern Syria. The IRGC prepares regiments of Houthi fighters, reaching as many as 100 elements in each unit.[32]

3. Arming and military assistance

Once the recruits complete the stage of training and preparation for warfare, they enter the phase of arming and doctrinal sup- port. They are ideologically energized to defend, to the last drop of blood, the Iranian project in the targeted countries. The arms shipments are sent to Iran-backed proxies and militias.

These entities receive sums of money, through the countries handling arming and military assistance, to buy weapons for the militias.[33]

» **Arms shipments for the Houthis**

The number of Iranian arms shipments for the Houthis seized on the Yemeni coast or in the vast deserts (outside of state con- trol) was approximately 15 from 2011-2018.[34] Three shipments were seized in 2017: the first October 1, 2017,[35] the second on October 21, 2017,[36] and the third on December 27, 2017.[37] The three shipments included an anti-tank missile, an artillery bat- tery, launch pads, and bombers. Moreover, other arms shipments were smuggled through the coastal town of Dhubab, 30 km North of Bab Mandeb; the strategic Mocha Port, 60 km North of Bab Mandab; and the ports of Hudaydah, like Khawkhah and the cen- tral port of Hudaydah.[38]

The Houthis have had armament systems, C-102, Fateh, Zelz- al, Burkan-1 missiles and the long-range Burkan-2 missile, which was launched towards Riyadh – the capital city of Saudi Arabia – in November 2017.[39] All the missiles are made in Iran. Annually, Iran sends to the Houthis sums of money amounting to about $20 million.

During a press conference held at the U.S. military base in Washington on December 13, 2017, the U.S. Ambassador to the United Nations, Nikki Haley, said that the pieces of the missile that the Houthis had fired against Saudi Arabia revealed that it was Iranian. This highlighted the fact that the Houthis had fired missiles at a civilian airport "with the potential to kill hundreds of innocent civilians." Haley said that the United States has evi- dence that Iran is assisting the Houthis with arms and missiles. She clarified that the U.N. resolutions bars Iran from selling or transferring weapons and missiles to the Houthis. Haley added that there has been no improvement in terms of Iran's actions or its continued support of terrorism. "It's hard to find a conflict or terror group in the Middle East that does not have Iran's finger- prints all over it," she said, stressing that Iran has been setting fire across the Middle East and that its violations have spread from Yemen, Lebanon, and Syria to Iraq and the United States, with "un- deniable" evidence in this regard. Haley called on the internation- al community to stand with the United States and confront Iran's threats before it becomes like North Korea, reaffirming that Iran's behavior violates the U.N. Security Council resolutions.[40] By the same token, the U.N. Secretary-General António Guterres stated, in a midterm report for the Panel of Experts, in regard to imposing sanctions on Iran, that the smuggled weapons to Yemen and the Iranian missiles were seemingly of "common origin."[41]

» Funding and arming militias in Syria

As of February 2018, international media outlets had never commonly confirmed the exact sums of money Iran sends to its militias and proxies in Syria, Iraq, Yemen, Lebanon, and Bahrain. A researcher at the Middle East Studies Center in Paris, Mohammad Amin, said that the IRGC allocated huge amounts of money for its proxy militias fighting in the Arab states, particularly in Syria. The 2017-2018 annual budget allocated more than $24.2 billion for military and security affairs – an amount equivalent to 23% of the state's overall budget – at the expense of the development sectors.[42]

In 2017, the National Council of Resistance of Iran (NCRI) published a book stating that the amount of money Iran sends annually to Syria is about $20 billion. Over the past five years, since the breakout of the Syrian crisis, Iran has spent $80-$100 billion. The Fares Center for Eastern Mediterranean Studies estimated that Iran spent a considerable annual sum in Syria: $17 billion. Of this, $15 billion was for the Syrian regime and $2 bil- lion was for the militias.[43] The United Nations has estimated that Iran spent $6 billion on 60 militias in Syria, whose members were recruited from Afghanistan, Pakistan, Yemen, and Iraq. [44] The Christian Science Monitor said that the Syrian regime receives $35 billion in financial support from Iran.[45]

The Mossad report, conducted by the Israeli intelligence expert Ronen Solomon in 2018, revealed that Iran transferred – through sea and land – weapons to fighters in Syria; to avoid being tracked by satellites, Iran made this transfer at night using Iranian civil- ian planes. Iran transferred 5,000s ton of weapons from Tehran and Abadan to Damascus; these were stored in its underground armory in Syria.[46] A BBC report on November 12, 2017, disclosed that Iran had established a huge military base in Southern Syria.[47] This clarified the reason for the continuous Israeli strikes target- ing Iran's stores of weapons distributed across Syria. It explained why an Iranian drone shot down an Israeli F16 jet after it crossed its Northern border with Syria in February 2018.[48]

Unit 190 – the Weapon Transfer Unit, one of the branches of the Quds Force – is assigned to transfer weapons to militias in Syria. It consists of several institutions and companies that serve as um- brella companies, hiding IRGC violations of the U.N. arms embar- go.[49]

The U.N. Security Council passed the following arms embargo resolutions: 1747 (2007), 1929 (2010), and 2105 (2013). The arms embargo included air-sea-land shipping companies that helped transfer fighters and weapons. One of these companies is Mahan Airlines. However, Iran, as usual, has been in non-com- pliance with the U.N. resolutions and has created new means to smuggle weapons.[50]

» **Arming the Lebanese Hezbollah**

Since its emergence in 1982, Hezbollah has received Iranian military assistance in becoming an unsurpassable power and a bargaining chip in the Lebanese political arena – one that can steer the Lebanese decision-making process in favor of Iran's project and the policies of Iran's allies. On November 23, 2017, the com- mander of the IRGC said that supplying Hezbollah with the most sophisticated weapons was non-negotiable.[51] A report published in September 2017 by the Foundation for Defense of Democracies, a non-profit and non-partisan policy institute, said that the Leba- nese Hezbollah receives $700-$800 million annually from Iran to fund its terror operations. The report revealed that Iran had been giving Hezbollah $100 million annually – an amount that, over the previous ten years, had increased to $200 million annually. The re- port concluded that Iran had increased its funding to the Lebanese Hezbollah militias to $700-$800 million during the period 2017- 2018.[52] Hezbollah now has Mohajer-4 drones and several types of missiles, whether made in or transported by Iran.[53] See table 3.

Table 3: The most significant Iranian handed to Hezbollah		
Model	Model	Model
Ra'ad	Zelzal	Katyusha
	C-802	Fajr-1, Fajr-2, Fajr-3, Artillery Rockets

Behind closed doors, the Israelis discuss the fact that Hezbol- lah possesses anti-tank missiles and the Iranian anti-tank guided missile Toophan-2.[54] The reports by Yedioth Ahronoth and Intelli- gence Online in September 2017 revealed that Hezbollah had es- tablished, with Iranian military, technical, and financial assistance, two weapons factories:

» The first factory is specialized in manufacturing light weapons and is in Zahrani in South Lebanon.
» The second factory is specialized in manufacturing long-range missiles and is in Hermel village in Baalbek, the stronghold of Hezbollah.[55]

There are two routes for transferring Iranian weapons to Hezbol- lah:

Land route: An internal route inside Lebanon, under Hezbollah control, is the easiest way to proceed logistically along Iran-Syr- ia-Lebanon roads. Weapons are transferred from Beqaa to Beirut, and finally, arrive in South Lebanon.

Air route: Planes take off from Iranian airports and land at Bei- rut International Airport. There, the arms shipments are unload- ed by Hezbollah, which controls the airport and its surrounding areas.

Israel has many assumptions about this type of shipping. The Israelis believe that Iran sends commercial airplanes loaded with weapons, or that Iran uses small military aircraft to transfer arms shipments to Hezbollah from the Syrian army's military bases to temporary airfields, established for a few hours, in Beqaa.[56]

» **Arming Shiite militias in Iraq:**

After the Iraqi leadership and the Public Mobilization Force (PMF) confessed – several times – to receiving Iranian arms supplies, the disclosure of the Iranian arms flow to its proxies became outdated. In May 2017, the Vice President of Iraq, Nouri Maliki, said, "The Iranian military assistance to Iraq in countering ISIS included arms and military expertise. Without it [military assis- tance] the Iraq Army would have collapsed and Baghdad would have fallen." His statement is blatant evidence of Iranian arms flow to Iraq.[57] In November 2017, the Head of the Security and Defense Committee in the Iraqi Parliament, Hakim Zamili, said that Iranian arms flow to Iraq has been unprecedented since the fall of Bagh- dad, clarifying that the arms transfer to the Shiite militias is traf- ficked through the Iraq-Iran border, which stretches for 150 km and has been under Iranian control since the toppling of Saddam Hussein in 2003.[58]

5. **Armed formations and organizations**

After the recruitment and arming of fighters from unstable countries and from Shiite communities in the targeted countries, the stage of formation begins. This stage is as simple as mobiliz- ing militia-sized groupings that bear arms to defend a regime loyal to the ruling power of these militia-sized groupings or to fight a disloyal regime that rejects the foreign plan. Iran has been form- ing loyal Shiite militias in Syria, Iraq, Lebanon, Yemen, and some Arabian Gulf states, exploiting them to implement its expansionist project.

The official statements of the commander of the IRGC, Moham- mad Ali Jafari, are blatant evidence of Iran's military involvement in the region. He said that his country sent "high-military officers to Syria." Also, in January 2016, he said, "There are around 200,000 IRGC-affiliated fighters in five states: Syria, Iraq, Yemen, Pakistan, and Afghanistan."[59] Former IRGC Commander Hossein Hamedani, killed in Syria in 2015, said in May 2014 that his country had con- tinued fighting in Syrian towns, revealing that Iran prepared to send 130,000 Basij fighters to support the Syrian regime's forces.[60] The Security and Defense

Committee in the Iraqi Parliament an- nounced in 2015 that it had documents confirming the presence of 30,000 Iranian fighters in Iraq.[61]

Iran officially announced that several generals and officers had been killed in regional conflicts. According to Iranian sources, the death toll for military and non-military fighters was around 2,700 during the period 2011-2017.[62] This number increased to 3,500 through October 2017.[63] Among the most important officers who were killed in the conflicts are Brigadier General Hamid Taqa-vi, killed in Iraq in December 2014,[64] and Commander Abdullah Khosravi of the Fatehin battalion (which defends Shiite shrines in Syria), who was killed in October 2017.[65] The secretary of Iran's Supreme National Security Council, Ali Shamkhani, said that if "people like Taqavi do not shed their blood in Samarra, then we would shed our blood [within Iran]."[66] In February 2016, Iran's Supreme Leader, Khamenei, praised those officers, saying, "They have sacrificed their souls there [Syria and Iraq], so enemies will not be able to get inside Iran. Without them, we would have been forced to confront the enemies in Kermanshah and Hamadān."[67]

a. **Holy Shrine Defenders:**[68] This is one of the most significant Iranian militias in Syria and Iraq. It is a transboundary group of Shiite fighters from elements of the IRGC, the Basij, the religious forces, and a number of marja' al-taqlid supporting Iran's Su- preme Leader Khamenei. Fifteen Shiite militia groups defend the holy shrines of Shiite Imams and their grandsons in Syria and Iraq. Iran describes the Holy Shrine Defenders as men who sacrifice their souls outside Iran to ensure security and stability in Syria and Iraq.[69] The group's name has a military meaning, though it is colored by religion. Its attached Shiite meaning represents the holy shrines in Najaf and Karbala in Iraq and the Sayedah Zainab shrine in Syria.[70] The Imam Hossein Base, an IRGC unit, is one of the most significant bases for the Holy Shrine Defenders. The in- formation available in this respect shows that the Imam Hossein Base operates the war in Syria and Iraq. Brigadier General Hossein Hamadani, a former commander of the base, said that the IRGC organized 70,000 Shiite and Alawite young men in Syria to fight in the war. Forty-two groups and 128 brigades are involved in the war in Syria, while 130,000 Basij fighters are waiting in Iran to participate in the war.[71]

Khamenei, while meeting with the families of the Holy Shrine Defenders, said, "They [the fighters] fought against the enemies, if they had not done that they should have fought them in Ker- manshah and the rest of [Iranian] governances." Qasem Soleimani said, "Defending Sayedah Zainab Shrine in Damascus is like de- fending the Shrine of Imam Hussein in Karbala ... I swear to Allah [God] defending Sayedah Zainab Shrine is like defending Imam Ali Holy Shrine and Imam Reza's shrine in Iran." He continued, "I swear to Allah, if Syria fell into the hands of takfereen [extrem- ists], they would demolish all holy sites of Ahl Al Bayt [the family of the prophet Mohammad]."[72] In February 2017, the Iranian Su- preme Leader's representative and preacher in Lorestan Province, Seyyed Ahmad Mir Emadi, said, "The holy shrine defenders were driven by Allah's power to fight outside the borders, defending the Islamic Iran and the Islamic world."[73] Ahmad Alamolhoda, leader of the Friday prayer of the province's capital, Mashhad, said, "We did not prevent wars by the nuclear deal and negotiations, but by the Holy Shrine Defenders. Without those holy shrine defenders, ISIS and America would have been in the heart of Iran ... the arro- gant powers tremble from the forces fighting in Iraq, and we have access to all the client-states of America in the region."[74]

b. **Armed popular mobilization:** The number of Shiite militias Iran formed in Iraq during the period 2003-2017 reached more than 61 armed militias, which all united under the Popular Mo- bilization Forces (PMF) at the end of 2016. The Supreme Lead- er of Iran ordered the merging of all the Shiite militias under one power, thereby duplicating Hezbollah's experience in Lebanon and completing the powerful group of its proxies across the Arab region, particularly in Iraq, Syria, and Yemen. PMF is led by Falih Alfayyadh and his deputy Abu Mahdi Almuhandis, an advisor and deputy of Qasem Soleimani. However, according to several media reports, the de-facto leader of PMF is Nouri Maliki.[75] No official statistics are available about the exact number of PMF fighters. Karim Nouri, spokesman for the PMF, said their number exceed- ed 130,000 fighters – equivalent to 15.5% of the total number of Iraqi Armed Forces (800,000: 250 in service and 550 reserve troops).[76] Iran pays the fighters monthly salaries ranging from $100 to $500.[77] Before the U.S. invasion of Iraq in 2003, militias such as the Badr Organization, led by Hadi Alameri, had emerged; after the fall of Baghdad, other militias had also formed. Howev- er, the largest number of militias arose after the emergence of ISIS in 2014. These included Asa'ib Ahl Haq, led by Qais Khazali; Harakat Hezbollah Nujaba, led by Akraam Kaabi; Kata'ib Hezbol- lah, the Mukhtar Army led by Wathiq Battat; the Abu Fadhel Abbas brigade, led by Aws Khafaji; Kata'ib Imam Ali, led by Shibl Zaydi,

Saraya Khorasani and the Abbas Division, led by Maytham Zaidi; and many other militias.[78] On December 14, 2017, the Iraqi marja' Ali Sistani called on the PMF to hand all the weapons it used in fighting "the extremists" to the Iraqi government, saying that the members of the armed militias were to be integrated with Iraqi security forces.[79] Sistani's call was thwarted by Iranian-Shiite re- jection. Qais Khazali, the commander of Asa'ib Ahl Haq, said that his organization is on course to establish what he called the Shiite Full Moon and not the Shiite Crescent. The spokesman of the PMF, Yousef Khalabi, said that the war against ISIS is not done; he said that while the military aspect has been completed, the process of countering radical ideology and terror organizations is ongoing. [80]

c. **Free Shiite Army**: The number of IRGC-affiliated militias in Syria is estimated at 100,000. They are recruited from Pakistani, Afghani, Lebanese, and Iraqi militias and directed by Qasem Solei- mani.[81] Most prominent among them is the Free Shiite Army, a transboundary military force that Iran formed in August 2016. It consists of:

- » Haidarioun brigade: Iraqi Shiites and Hezbollah battalions.
- » Fatimiyoun brigade: Afghani Shiites.
- » Zaynabioun brigade: Pakistani Shiites.[82]

It is reported that the number of IRGC fighters in Syria is es- timated at 8,000 and 6,000 from the regular Iranian Army, dis- patched across areas of conflict and strategic geographical terri- tories to spread their dominance, thereby smoothing the path for the Iranian project.[83] The commander Qasem Soleimani directs the military operations in Syria and Iraq along with his deputy in the Quds Force, Brigadier General Ismael Qani, who runs the IRGC military operations in Aleppo and its countryside, and Brigadier General Rostam Qasemi, who heads the Guards' construction con- glomerate in Damascus and its outskirts.

The visit of the Iranian military's Chief of Staff, Major Gener- al Mohammad Bagheri, to Syria on December 17, 2017, cannot pass unnoticed. His visit was intended to secure Iran's role as a key player in the future of post-ISIS Syria by protecting Iranian military areas in its sphere of influence and to deeply root armed militias across Syria.[84]

d. **Ansarullah:** During the 1980s, Iran supported the armed An- sar Allah militia, commonly known as the Houthis, led by Hus- sein Badreddin Houthi. After his death in the 2004 Sa'dah War, his father, Badreddin Houthi, led the militia during the period 2004-2006. Since 2006, the Houthis have been led by his brother, Abdul-Malik Badreddin Houthi. All the Houthi leaders had lived in Iran during the 1990s and were influenced by Twelver Shiism because they belonged to Jaroudiah, the Shiite sect ideologically closest to the Twelvers.[85]

e. **Lebanese Hezbollah:** Iran formed Hezbollah in 1982 as an armed militia. It is one of the strongest armed proxies Iran uses to implement its expansionist project in the region, particularly in Lebanon, because it is located within the Shiite Crescent. In 2016, Hezbollah commanded an estimated 20,000 active troops and 25,000 reservists. The group receives military training from the IRGC. Iran helps Hezbollah establish armed parties in Yemen, Iraq, Syria, Kuwait, Bahrain, and Saudi Arabia. These parties have carried out terror attacks in the Arabian Gulf region, destabilizing regional security.[86]

Conclusion:

1. Since the 1979 revolution, the theocratic regime has been em- bedding military alignments into Shiism, i.e., making the military one of the pillars of Shiism. Also, it has been using the military as a crucial and influential element in promoting the ideology of velayet-e faqih, or "Exporting the Revolution" – a term com- monly used by Iranian revolutionists and officially listed in the Iranian Constitution. By emotionally motivating the people in the region (particularly the Arab region), Iran paves the way for its regional proxies, whether religious or military, to cross the Arab region and many other regions around the world.

2. Iran uses various effective tools in militarizing Shiism. It gives military training to Shiite minorities in Arab and non-Arab re- gions. This training includes the use of arms in battle and indoc- trination into military life. Thus, Shiite minorities become com- petent enough to implement Iran's expansionist project across the region.

3. Iran gives the military, bases, units, formations, IRGC brigades, and colleges Shiite names with doctrinal meaning. It creates a belief, support, and doctrinal loyalty among members of the military and citizens, generating strong grassroots support that decision-makers can instrumentally use as a bargaining chip to spread influence and generate legitimacy for the Iranian regime. Therefore, the Iranian regime can more strongly confront the regional and international calls against its expansionist project. Eventually, the military members and personnel of the IRGC will be harmoniously merged by their Shiite doctrine and will de- fend, with all the power they have, the policies and agendas of the IRGC, both at home and abroad.

4. Militarization is the third stage of the Iranian process of Shii- fication. The earlier two stages are Soft Shiism (spreading the Twelver Shia doctrine through soft power tools) and politiciz- ing Shiism (politicizing the Shiite enclaves and pushing them to generate Iran-backed political movements whose orientations are different from those of ruling systems, with the goal being to implement the Iranian agendas). Later, the Shiite militias are integrated into the national armies.

Endnotes

(1) *Meriam-Webster Dictionary*. Accessed April 2017,24. https://bit.ly/2HU3Ngd.

(2) Kazem, Alamdari. "The Power Structure of the Islamic Republic of Iran: Transition from Populism to Clientelism, and Militarization of the Government." *Third World Quarterly* 26, no. 301-285: (2005) 8. http://cutt. us/yHsvD. See also, Saleh, Adnan, "Militarization of Statehood Gnaws Construction of Modern Statehood," http://cutt.us/ jH9dj.

Shiism, in the Arabic language, means "prevailed," being loyal and a follower. If someone converts to Shiite Islam, he becomes Shiite. Originally, Shiites were those who became loyal to Ali bin Abi Talib and claimed that he is the most deserving of the Caliphate amongst the other three of Prophet Mohammad's companions: Abu Bakr, Omar Ibn

Al-Khatab, and Othman bin Afan. Later, they were divided into multiple sects of different doctrines.

(3) "Mapping the Global Muslim Population." Power Research Center. http:// cutt.us/ Ou54Q.

(4) "World Factbook." CIA. Accessed April 2018,24. http://cutt.us/NqvC7.

(5) "Sunnis and Shia: Islam›s Ancient Schism." BBC. January 2016,4. http://cutt. us/3VASk.

(6) CIA, op. cit.

(7) Power Research Center, op. cit.

(8) Talat, Ramih. "Militarizing Shiism." *Alrased*, no. 51. January 2016,10. http:// cutt.us/ NDhkE.

(9) Mohammed, Alsulami. "Iran and Militarizing Shiism." *Alwatan*. April 2017,5. http:// cutt.us/EpKZj.

* *Maddahis*, the plural form of *maddah*, is a specialized ceremonial singer usually performed during Shiite religious ceremonies.

(10) Mohammed, Alsulami, and Abdulraouf Alghoneimi. *The Shiite Geopolitics: Present and Future*. Riyadh: AGCIS, 2017.

(11) Alsulami, op. cit.

(12) Mahjoob, Alzuwairi,. "Doctrinal Burden: Factors Ruling Iranian Policy Toward the Arab World." *Al Siyassa Al Dawliya*, March 2015,15. http://cutt.us/xdCLf.

(13) Hussein, Salami. "Our Capabilities Geographically Stretch to the Middle East." *Fars News*, n.d. http://cutt.us/WBDgo.

(14) Hambi, Obaid. "Reading in the Strategy of Spread Shiism and the Functional Role of Iran in the American Strategy." *Iran News*, April 2018,26. http://cutt.us/WKsB4

(15) Alsulami and Alghoneimi, op. cit.

(16) "Islamic Revolutionary Guard Corps (IRGC)." Counter Extremism. Accessed April,27 2018.) http://cutt.us/gBXle.

(17) Feras, Elias. "Iranian Military Doctrine." *Washington Institute*. November 2017,15. http://www.washingtoninstitute.org/fikraforum/view/iranian-military-doctrine.

(18) Alsulami, op. cit.

(19) Ibid.

(20) "9 Major Maneuvers Conducted in 7 Months." November 2017,4. http://cutt.us/wa3P8.

(21) "Denial of Jum›a Imam of Amol, Jalil Murtazavi›s Death in Syria." Adalat Khahan. March 2017. http://cutt.us/A6qDT.

(22) "Iranian Shia Eulogists Dispatched to Damascus to Wage Propaganda War for Tehran." Rasanah IIIS. October 2016,27. http://cutt.us/ScHg.

(23) "Iranian Maddahis Express Support for the Forces Stationed at the Front in Syria." Reuters. March 2016,28. http://cutt.us/nXHsn.

(24) Ibid.

(25) "Who Are Appointed by Iran's Supreme Leader." Reuters. Translated by Rasanah IIIS. May 2016,10. http://cutt.us/XXzDl.

(26) Kenneth, Katzman. The IRGC: *Emergence, Formation, and Role*. Abu Dhabi: Emirates Center for Strategic Studies and Research, 1996.

(27) Ramih, op. cit.

(28) Alsulami, op. cit.

(29) Ibid., and see: Fadel, Salwa. "When Will the Global Shiite Army Emerge?" *Janoubia*, December 2016,5.

(30) "Salami Admits: Pakistanis, Afghans, and Indians are fighting in Syria." Tasnim Agency. Translated by Rasanah IIIS. December 2017,11. http://cutt.us/RRK0H.

(31) Eri, Shaw. "Opposition Group Claims Iran Sponsoring New Terror Training Camps." Fox News, February 2017,15. http://cutt.us/s9z3S.

(32) "IRGC Garrisons for Training Terrorists Around the World: Detailed Report." Yemen Press, January 2016,22. http://cutt.us/6t0vO.

(33) "From Gaza to Yemen, Syria, Lebanon, and Iraq, This Is What Tehran Spends on the Middle East Project." Lebanese-forces. January 2018,15. http://cutt.us/zlmvb.

(34) Madbash, Arafat. "The Coalition Counters Iranian Ship Heading to Houthis and Loaded with Arms." Asharq al-Awsat. October 2015,1. http://cutt.us/zRdYV.

(35) "Iranian Smuggling Ship Seized in Yemeni Water." Sky News Arabia. October,21 2017. http://cutt.us/4DHdh.

(36) "The Coalition Announces Seizing Arms Iran Smuggled to Houthis." Sky News Arabia. December 2017,27. http://cutt.us/Xd9Lv.

(37) "Yemen: The Coalition Intercepts Two Boats Loaded with Arms for Militias." Alsjl. November 2016,16. http://cutt.us/kdnby.

(38) "Saudi Arabia Intercepts a Ballistic Missile near Riyadh." November 2017,5. http:// cutt.us/wxzOM.

(39) Lebanese-forces, op. cit.

(40) "Haley: Iran Is Involved in Targeting Saudi Arabia with Ballistic Missiles." Al Arabiya. December 2015,15. http://cutt.us/d9XMU.

(41) "Haley: I Will Provide Blatant Evidence of Iran's Supplying the Houthis with Missiles." Rasanah IIIS. December 2017,13. http://cutt.us/FDxhL.

(42) Omar Haj, Hassan. "Iran Spends 24$ Billion Annually to Support Its Militias in Arab States." Baladi News. May 2017,10. http://cutt.us/ppVFP.

(43) Lebanese-forces, op. cit.

(44) "Iranian Regime Spends Billions of Dollars for the Expenditures of Militias in Syria." People's Mojahedin Organization of Iran. June 2017,1. http://cutt.us/M8gir.

(45) "The Strategy of Iran and Russia in Syria." *Nedaa Syria*. June 2017,22. http://cutt.us/ ZIRwm.

(46) Sami, Khalifa. "The Mossad Report of the Night Activity of Hezbollah and Iran in Syria," Almodon. August 2017,28. http://cutt.us/SKDsz.

(47) "BBC: Iran Establishes a Military Base in Southern Damascus." RT. November,10 2017. http://cutt.us/D3J3B.

(48) "Israel Shuts Down Iranian Drone, Israeli F16 Downed." *Aliwaa*. February 2018,10. http://cutt.us/nZP6h.

(49) Pollak, Nadav. "Rethinking U.S. Strategy for Intercepting Iranian Arms Transfers." Washington Institute. August 2015,20. http://cutt.us/42i4d.

(50) "Iranian Civilian Flights of False Numbers Transfer Arms to Damascus." Asharq al- Awsat. August 2016,28. http://cutt.us/eAjUK.

(51) Mettri, Said. "Tehran: Supplying Hezbollah with the Best Arms is Unnegotiable." RT. November 2017,23. http://cutt.us/Z829.

(52) "Report: Iran Funds Hezbollah with 800-700$ Million Annually." Almnatiq. January 2018,25. http://cutt.us/Zbc0v.

(53) Michelle, Nassre. "Between Lebanese Air Force and Hezbollah's Drones." Bintjbeil. September 2014,29. http://cutt.us/F0w4l.

(54) "Mossad's Data on Hezbollah's Weapons." Alwatan Voice. October 2006,13. http:// cutt.us/Ml0Og.

(55) Soha, Jaffal. "Hezbollah's Factories: Missiles in Zahrani and Hermel and Chemical Weapons in Rural Hama." September 2017,7. hhttp://cutt.us/vU4z5

(56) Hussein, Samoor. "A Military Road Map Between Iran and Hezbollah." Sputnik News. August 2017,15. http://cutt.us/dljzg.

(57) Ibrahim, Obaidi. "Biggest Terrorist Army: Militia Locusts Invade the World." Baghdad Post. May 2017,22. http://cutt.us/BGsnV.

(58) Rinad, Mansoor, and Abduljabar, Fahel. "PMF and Future of Iraq." Carnegie Middle East Center. April 2017,28. http://cutt.us/aF7CA.

(59) Adel, Alsalemi. "The Commander of IRGC Admits 200,000 Fighters Deployed in Five Countries." Asharq al-Awsat. January 2016,14. http://cutt.us/AMTII.

(60) "The Iranian General Who Saved Assad and Established the Syrian Hezbollah is Killed." Annahar. October 2015,9. http://cutt.us/YrGj6.

(61) Salah, Abdulatif. "Iranian Interventions in Iraq: History, Reality and Future." Masr- Alarabia. March 2015,30. http://cutt.us/juMvl.

(62) Behnam, Gholipour. "Deaths in Iraq Show Two Sides of Iran's Role in Sectarian Conflict." The Guardian. December 2014,30, https://bit.ly/2JvhhMT

(63) Saleh, Hamid. "11 Killed from Iran and Its Militias." Al Arabiya. October 2017,23. http://cutt.us/ELeal.

(64) "Funeral of the Brigadier General Hamid Taqavi, a Commander in IRGC, Who was Killed in Iraq." Elnashra. December 2014,29. http://cutt.us/7GPLn.

(65) "Funeral of Six Iranian Soldiers Killed in Syria." Pishkhaan. October 2017,2. http:// cutt.us/hsCwj.

(66) "Washington Turns Away, Leaving Iraq for Iran." Erem News. June 2016,2. http://cutt.us/jhCoT.

(67) "Khamenei Defends Iran's Military Intervention in Syria." Al Arabiya. February,5 2016. http://cutt.us/FZsvm.

(68) The Holy Shrine or Haram, according to Shiite doctrine, consists of the shrines of the Prophet Mohammad's family in Syria and Iraq.

(69) Herad, Talou'i. "From Where the Defenders of the Shrine Come?" Radio Zamaneh. September 2017,26. http://cutt.us/vHqS4.

(70) Abdulghani, Kaker. "Iranian Packed Militias Recruit Pakistanis and Afghanis for the Syrian War." Salam Times. February 2017,28. http://cutt.us/fXHp9.

(71) "15 Groups Fighting in Syria and Iraq on Behalf of Iran." http://cutt.us/uNuPR.

(72) Ibid., Herad Talou'i, http://cutt.us/vHqS.

(73) "Representative of the Supreme Leader in Lorestan and Friday Prayer's Leader in Khorramabad Seyyed Ahmad Mir Emadi." IRNA News Agency. http://cutt.us/EqrDG

(74) Ibid., Herad Talou'i, http://cutt.us/vHqS.

(75) Iraqi, Mohammad. "Iran and the Future of Armed Militias in the Post-ISIS Iraq." *Journal for Iranian Studies 3* (2017). http://cutt.us/ZuOiy.

(76) Mahmoud, Abu Baker. "PMF: From Unorganized Factions to Official Military Formation." BBC. February 2017,23. http://cutt.us/6HuO8.

(77) "Washington Times Unveils in Numbers the Iranian Financial Support for Assad." Orient News. September 2015,6. http://cutt.us/xwgVh.

(78) Ibrahim, Obaidi, op. cit.

(79) "Sistani Calls on for Disarming and Integrating the Shiite Militiamen into Iraqi Security Forces." Alsouria. December 2017,15. http://cutt.us/vp5Gw.

(80) Mohammad, Abdullah. "After Sistani's Call, Will the PMF Hand Its Weapons to the Government?" Roayah News. December 2017,16. http://cutt.us/7FUQS.

(81) Saleh, Hamid. "A Report Unveils New Information About Iranian Militias in Syria." Al Arabiya. October 2017,11. http://cutt.us/2DgTN.

(82) "Iran Officially Announces Forming the Transboundary 'Free Shiite Army' Led by Major General Qasem Soleimani." Tunisia Now. August 2016,19.

(83) Department of Political Analysis. "Strategy of Iran and Russia in Syria." Eldorar. January 2017,31. http://cutt.us/hiX9w.

(84) Saleh, Hamid. "After Soleimani Iran's Commander in Chief in Aleppo Threats the Opposition." Al Arabiya. October 2017,20. http://cutt.us/J2guV.

(85) Jamal, Abu Hussien. "Ansar Allah Organization (the Houthis), Its Doctrinal Formation and Political Battles." Al Siyassa Al Dawliya. August 2014,31. http://cutt.us/2kMJA.

(86) *Rifle of Supreme Jurist Leader: Hezbollah in Lebanon.* Dubai: Al-Mesbar Studies and Research Center, .25-9,2017

An Assessment of the Iranian Military Doctrine and Military Leadership Developments, Obstacles, and Prospects for Change

Alex Vatanka (Ph.D.)
Senior Fellow at the Middle East Institute, Washington D.C.

Introduction

There can be no doubt that despite much speculation about Washington's long-term intentions, the United States remains the most powerful political-military actor in the Middle East. In that context, the most formidable adversary of the US in the region is the Islamic Republic of Iran. A self-declared enemy of the US, Iran is today busy weighing its options as it seeks to maximize its influ- ence in the Middle East and beyond. This Iranian pursuit of power is occurring on different levels and involves different Iranian re- gime actors. However, one of the most significant actors – if not the most significant – is the Iranian military and specifically the Islamic Revolution Guards Corps (IRGC). The focus of this analysis paper is an assessment of the latest developments involving Iran's military developments, its agenda, and the obstacles it is facing or likely will have to tackle.

1. The debate about the Iranian military

In the United States, after 16 years of ongoing military opera- tions in the Middle East, American military planners are confront- ed with a simple but powerful reality: that US national security in- terests will force Washington to remain engaged in Middle Eastern affairs in the foreseeable future.[1] On an operational level, military engagement against anti-American forces will continue to be re- quired in some of the most sensitive spots in the region, including Afghanistan, Iraq, Syria, and Yemen.

In this context, the US is not confronting a single conventional military power (as with Saddam Hussein's Iraq in 1990). Instead, the US is faced with the prospects of cases of 'hybrid war,' which is essentially a combination of conventional military assets, ter- rorist/militia operations, cyber warfare, and disinformation me- dia campaigns. Here, among America's foes, the Iranian threat is unique.[2]

The Iranians know full well that regarding conventional military capabilities they are woefully behind not only the United States but also other US allies such as Saudi Arabia, Israel, and the United Arab Emirates. Most notably, Iran's air force and naval capabilities are no match for its adversaries. In fact, one can argue that Iran has only two vital military assets: its 'asymmetric warfighting' and its growing missile arsenal.[3] Nonetheless, military planners in Tehran are known to exploit an array of military tools to bolster Iran's ability to project power.

The motivations behind Iran's emphasis on 'asymmetric' capa- bilities were initially out of necessity. However, this type of mil- itary modus operandi has since 2011 gained additional signif- icance for Tehran thanks to opportunities that emerged on the regional scene. After Iran's revolution of 1979, when the

United States ceased to be Iran's principal supplier of military hardware, training, and advice, the regime in Tehran had no choice but to im- provise as it looked to address its military deficiencies.[4]

Two of Iran's present-day military strengths – its use of foreign proxy groups and its development of a missile arsenal – emerged as policy priorities in the immediate period after the 1979 revo- lution and intensified during the Iran-Iraq War (1980-1988). The onset of the Arab revolts from 2011, combined with the emergence of ISIS [Daesh] in 2014, has since given Iran ample opportunities to look for ways to further intervene militarily outside of its bor- ders, which it has pursued with notable (but also controversial) intensity.

Nonetheless, the question is whether these latest Iranian mil- itary interventions in the region amount to a new offensive 'mil- itary doctrine' as such or if they are merely a reflection of Iranian opportunism in the face of power vacuums created in a number of states due to social upheavals resulting from popular Arab re- volts.[5] This question cannot be conclusively answered at the mo- ment given the lack of data but there can be little doubt that avail- able empirical evidence does suggest the Iranians are evaluating a broad range of military policy options for the future.

At the same time, it is important not to assume a full consensus to exist in Tehran on the question of the country's military posture. The Iranian regime is deliberately set up in a way to pit various state organs against each other as, for example, the IRGC against the Artesh (regular armed forces) or the President and his gov- ernment against the Office of the Supreme Leader. However, while this division of labor together with intra-regime rivalry for power makes it hard to predict Tehran's next military moves, specific re- cent developments point to an IRGC-led effort toward establishing an agiler offensive doctrine.

2. The consolidation of the 'asymmetric doctrine.'

In his March 2017 statement, the head of the US Central Com- mand, General Joseph Votel, stated:

> "We continue to see malign Iranian influence across Iraq and Syria. While they currently are focused on countering ISIS in Iraq, we remain concerned about Iran's efforts to prop up the Syrian regime against the opposition and its desire to exploit Shia population centers to increase their malign influence, not just in Syria, but also in Arab states across the region. This supports their long-term aspiration to achieve regional hegemony. Moreover, we are watching closely for indications and warnings of decreasing Iranian concern regarding the threat posed by ISIS, leading to a potential shift to targeting

U.S. and coalition personnel and infrastructure to influence a
potential long-term U.S. security presence. Furthermore, we
must take care to ensure that our actions do not unintentionally
strengthen the Iranian position within the region."[6]

This was the most critical assessment about Iran made by a se- nior
American military official in recent years. Still, and notwith- standing the usual
Iranian bluster, Tehran's response to Votel was relatively mute. The reasons for
this Iranian silence can be due to different factors, but one such factor is very
likely a desire by the Iranian leadership not to provoke the American generals.

The Iranians have concluded that US military officials – such as James
Mattis in the Pentagon – have an unprecedented degree of influence in the
foreign policy decision-making process (particu- larly on questions relating
to the Middle East) in the Trump ad- ministration and should not be overly
provoked. For example, as soon as Trump entered the White House, the US
military reported a reduction in the IRGC navy's harassment of American ships
in the Gulf.

In other words, the silence against Votel seems to be part of a deliberate
decision in Tehran not to provoke the military estab- lishment in the United
States since they have an apparent ability to determine President Trump's future
policy toward Iran. Mean- while, the Iranian regime's present assessment appears
to be that the White House, and the National Security Council, in particular, are
advocates of a more hawkish policy toward Iran and are open to the idea of
military confrontation against Tehran, while the Pen- tagon is as of today still
hesitant to launch an open-ended military campaign against Iran.[7]

Recent reports in the United States suggest that in the armed skirmishes
in eastern Syria, for example, it is the Pentagon that is reluctant to expand its
anti-Iran military operations. The reason is mainly that the US military still sees
itself as inherently unpre- pared to confidently confront Iran's 'asymmetric'
arsenal. The Ira- nians recognize this reality and the Pentagon's assessment and
are hence unwilling to jeopardize this advantage needlessly.

The Martyrdom State Conception

The Iranian regime likes to show itself as a martyrdom-seeking state. In
reality, Iran's military strategy remains mostly very cau- tious. For example, in
the case of Syria, Tehran has been cautious in the numbers of troops it has been
willing to deploy to the bat- tlefields. In fact, since the conclusion of the Iran-Iraq
War in 1988, Tehran's military strategy has been overwhelmingly about avoid-
ing a head-on conventional military collision with its principal in- ternational
and regional adversaries such as the United States.[8]

However, as IRGC commanders are keen to repeat, the shifting regional security environment requires for Iran's military strate- gy to adapt and to reinvent itself. In Tehran, this is often referred to 'forward defense' and the idea that Iran should battle its oppo- nents outside its borders to prevent conflict from taking place on Iranian soil.[9]

This kind of military restitution necessitates plenty of readjust- ments, including the conversion of some of the existing regular military units.

Meanwhile, it is in the Artesh (regular conscript armed forces) where the Iranians have the most potential for a transformation.

The Artesh is, in terms of size, (approximately 350,000) about three times bigger than the IRGC (approximately 120,000). Artesh units are mostly organized in heavy armored infantry and mecha- nized units, which are distinctly a legacy of defense planning from the days of the Shah when the United States helped Iran plan for major conventional ground battles against the likes of the Soviet Union and Saddam Hussein's Iraq.

Today, there is almost no prospect for such ground-based mili- tary battles between Iran and its closest adversaries. As is current- ly evident, Iran's two most intense regional rivalries with Saudi Arabia and Israel are overwhelmingly happening via proxy actions and not through direct conventional military confrontation.

Accordingly, some military planners in Tehran appear to con- sider the Artesh's present capabilities as being a misfit and inap- propriate for Iran's foreign policy ambitions in the region in places such as Syria. By converting some Artesh manpower for so-called 'forward operations,' the battle-hardened IRGC military units can be made more readily available for domestic security operations inside the Islamic Republic should circumstances require it. One example is a 2009 type of Green opposition movement rising up again, requiring suppression.

In other words, if Iran opts for a major military makeover, it is in the realm of the Artesh where it will find most flexibility and space for change and reform.

However, while the concept of 'forward defense' on a large mili- tary scale is something of a new idea, the use of asymmetric tactics is as old as the Islamic Republic. To overcome its conventional mil- itary weakness following the cut in US military supplies to Iran in 1980, and also given Tehran's limited financial capacity to engage in major military procurement, the Iranians have for some nearly 40 years relied disproportionately on low-cost deterrence to pro- tect the homeland.

This process began in the 1980s during the war with Iraq. It was at this time that the Iranians began to focus on and develop asymmetric capabilities, including the formation of Iraqi (and later Af- ghan) proxies, short, medium

*An Assessment of the Iranian Military Doctrine and Military
Leadership Developments, Obstacles, and Prospects for Change*

|133

and long-range missiles, and mining and other anti-access and area-denial operations in the Gulf.

Iran's latest declarations of a new 'forward-defense' strategy are in fact only an extension of a process that has been in motion for many years. The significant difference is that Iran now can launch such asymmetric efforts on a scale unseen before thanks to a power vacuum found in so many conflict areas in the broader Middle East. Iranian operations in Iraq and Syria since 2012 and 2014 respectively are the best examples of this new reality.

Changing the Military Tactic

In terms of specific signals that might substantiate such reform of the Iranian military doctrine, one could point to the April 2017 statement by Kiumars Heydari,[10] the head of the Ground Forces of the Artesh (Iranian conscript armed forces). Heydari said that some of the units under his command are to be transformed into 'offensive' forces that can be deployed frontally outside of Iran's borders.

The exact motivation behind the statement is unclear, but two facts are not in dispute:

Heydari is a former IRGC commander who was appointed to the Artesh command role only in November 2016 by Ayatollah Ali Khamenei.

Furthermore, there are plenty of indications that the historic rivalry between the Artesh and IRGC is still ongoing. The deploy- ment of 'offensive' forces is traditionally the area of operation of the IRGC and not the Artesh. If Heydari's promise proves to be true, then the implication is that the IRGC is shaping the Artesh in its own image. This is an critical unfolding reorganization.

It represents a significant development but it is not a surprise as such. The IRGC overwhelmingly shapes Tehran's regional mili- tary posture and operations and it has a clear preference for the use of proxies.[11] This is both relatively inexpensive for Iran, and it provides considerable scope for deniability for the IRGC and its controversial actions. In fact, someone as central in Iran's regional military planning as Qassem Soleimani (head of Iran's Qods Force) knows best how to wage warfare via militant Iran controls.

A relevant example of this was the IRGC's operations against the US military in Iraq from 2003 to 2010. While the US detected the hand of the IRGC, the fact that the Iranians relied on Iraqi proxy groups for the attacks on the US provided Iran with enough deni- ability that Iran was able to avoid a direct US response. Limiting the IRGC's scope of deniability must be a key goal for any adver- sary of the IRGC.

This *modus operandi* means that Iran relies heavily on Arab prox- ies. This is relatively low-cost and gives Tehran deniability but it is a double-edged sword.

On the one hand, the IRGC already has vast experience with forming proxies that look to it for ideological guidance and military-financial support. The list includes groups such as Lebanese Hezbollah, the Iraqi Badr Corps or Asaib Ahl Al-Haq, various Afghan groups and to some extent even the Yeme- ni Houthis. Iran can be expected to continue to work along these lines based on a tested formula. IRGC will look for a security vacu- um in the region and will fill it to the extent that it can, however, it will not push its luck by being too dogmatic in steering the prox- ies it selects and will work with what it has at hand.

On the other hand, the IRGC faces the danger of over-reliance on proxies as there is always an inherent danger in such groups act- ing unilaterally or even against Tehran's wishes. The cases of Hez- bollah's 2006 war with Israel (which Iran had initially opposed), or the 2011 decision by Hamas to abandon Bashar Al Assad, are two good examples of Tehran being wrong-footed by proxy allies.

Finally, while the Iranians demonstrate strategic patience in many of their regional military operations, there is always an in- herent danger of overreach by doing too much too fast thanks to the multiple fronts that have opened up in the Middle East since 2011.

The IRGC leadership recognizes that the organization's Achilles heel is the perception among the Iranian population that its ad- venturist actions are costing the nation dearly or risking severe retaliation.

Its nervousness on this front was evident in late April 2017 when a number of public figures in Iran criticised Iran's Syria policy. Ali Saeedi, Khamenei's personal representative in the IRGC, was forced to portray the organization as the first-line of defense of the Iranian nation.[12] The incident apparently demonstrated the IRGC's anxiety about a backlash among Iranians, which will also shape its future calculations.

Meanwhile, despite the lack of data, what is certain is that the IRGC has been experimenting with various new ways of warfare for some time and the latest statements about a potential reorga- nization of the Artesh Ground Forces has to be seen in the context of this evolving thinking. What is beyond doubt is that the use of local proxies will continue to be the preferred modus operandi of the IRGC in the areas of conflict where it is militarily involved. Accordingly, major Iranian rearmament of its conventional forces, a costly proposition, is improbable in the foreseeable future.

Finally, it is imperative that Tehran's effort in the realm of military planning is not judged against military objectives only. Its asym- metric warfare capacities act as deterrents against Iran's rivals, as most vividly demonstrated by the hesitation it has generated in- side the Pentagon about what to do with the Iranian threat. How- ever, Tehran's cultivation of Arab proxies is also a way of creating political leverage inside state institutions in targeted countries such as

Iraq, Syria, and Yemen. These proxies have a proven re- cord to eventually become mouthpieces for Iran's broader ideo- logical agenda, and the implications of such political propagation will last much longer than Iran's military agenda.

3. The centrality of missiles

Besides 'asymmetric' capabilities, Tehran also takes pride in and invests a considerable amount in financially supporting and diplomatically defending its missiles program. In fact, in its first clash with Iran in January 2017, the Trump administration was faced with Iran test-firing a ballistic missile. It was Iran's way of declaring its commitment to its missiles as its 'red line' and that it was unwilling to make any concessions in this field.[13]

However, the US Congress has a number of new sanctions pro- posals under considerations, and they target Iran's missile arsenal.

It remains to be seen whether these new sanctions will be imple- mented and what the US Defense Department will recommend to President Trump about the challenge of Iran. The Obama adminis- tration was of the view that the Iranian missile arsenal was a 'man- ageable' risk as long as they could not deliver nuclear weapons.

As of today, the international community appears reluctant to link Iran's missile program to other questions such as the sustain- ability of the 2015 nuclear agreement or Tehran's regional agenda. In other words, unless the US can mobilize international support, the Iranian missile program will continue to advance and is un- likely to be the reason for further penalties against Tehran by the international community.

In fact, the muted international response to Iran's launch of six ballistic missiles against ISIS in Syria in June is an indication that Tehran's missiles are not presently a mobilizing factor for the in- ternational community.

At this point, it should be remembered how prized the missile program is to the IRGC. The organization revealed a new missile facility on 25 May 2017. It did so only a few hours before the US Senate was to vote on new sanctions against Iran. It was a message by the IRGC generals that its missiles are non-negotiable. This is the third officially acknowledged underground facility under the control of the IRGC that produces ballistic missiles.

What is unknown is whether the IRGC announcement had been coordinated beforehand with the Presidential Palace or the For- eign Ministry. However, during the election, Hassan Rouhani re- peatedly criticised the IRGC for the way in which it adopts con- frontationist postures to undermine the Rouhani government's outreach to the world.

At the time, there was very little open criticism of the IRGC an- nouncement or the timing behind it in Iran. Regarding subtle crit- icism, pro-Rouhani outlets such as Donya-e Eqtesad did so only indirectly by referring to the anxiety the IRGC announcement has created outside of Iran. In many ways, the US Senate's timing to vote on a new set of sanctions on Iran was timely for the generals of the IRGC. As it came right after the 19 May Iranian elections and Rouhani's massive victory, the IRGC announcement about a new missile facility was not only a signal to the Americans but also to the Rouhani government that the president's win in the elections will not change the first calculations of the IRGC.

4. The role of Iran's foreign partners

The Iranian leadership prioritizes two foreign states as priority military partners; China and Russia. Both states have played an instrumental role in the last few decades in assisting Iran's in- digenous military production capabilities (such as missiles) and often share Iran's regional interests as in Iraq and Syria. However, much of the latest military-to-military cooperation between Iran and Russia and China has not been directly linked to enhancing the quality of Tehran's military abilities but are mostly rooted in a desire on the part of the Iranians to show themselves as able to cultivate alternative global players as partners.[14]

A good example of this is the recent return of Chinese mili- tary vessels to Iran, which Tehran hailed as a sign that its mil- itary-to-military cooperation with Beijing is moving ahead as planned. The last time Chinese warships docked in Iran was in 2014, and it was then that the two states had their first-ever joint military exercises.

The drills, which were conducted in the Sea of Oman and east to the Strait of Hormuz, involved about 700 naval forces from each country and can be described as some of the most extensive naval exercises Iran has conducted jointly with a foreign power in recent years. Involving Iranian and Chinese destroyers and anti-submarine helicopters, the Iranian side has been promising closer military cooperation with China since at least November 2016.[15]

It was then that the Chief of Staff of Iran's Armed Forces, Mo- hammad Bagheri, said that nothing would be in the way of foster- ing 'strategic military ties with China.' However, the Iranian side is careful not to present the latest military cooperation as targeting any third-state (such the United States or the Arab Gulf States) as Tehran knows full well that China will not want to engage on the side of Iran in Middle Eastern rivalries. Instead, the closer military ties are presented merely as a way of protecting the vast commercial trade that the two states carry out each year.

As long as Iran markets its military engagements with foreign partners to be defensive in nature, the criticism against such mil- itary drills from Western states will be limited.

Still, the latest Iranian defense dealings with Russia and China are creating a great deal of speculation in Washington. In Tehran, there is talk of a $10 billion arms deal with Russia and more and even closer defense cooperation with China. There is even talk of the Hamadan Air Base again becoming available for the Russians for operations in Syria.[16] The question arises as to how to explain this latest build up in Iranian defense talks with Russia and China, as well as the timing thereof.

In both cases, the arrival of President Trump has something to do with it. Certainly, Iran and Russia have been talking about closer military cooperation dating back many years. Such talks become even more visible after 2014 and the Ukraine crisis. The same happened with the Chinese from 2014. Talks with China and Russia by Iranian defense officials are always presented as 'strategic.' Two things are important to remember in this context: With the Russians, Iran has a real military need to import hard- ware and parts. This is particularly true in the field of air and air defense. However, this does not in itself amount to 'strategic' de- fense cooperation as such. Meanwhile, the Iranians are still suspi- cious of Russia and its agenda.

Secondly, with China, there is also suspicion (particularly as Beijing is believed to be against Iran's membership in the Shang- hai Cooperation Organisation). Still, Iran sees China's military build-up as a protector of Chinese-backed infrastructure projects, which Iran is both party to and benefits from. Look, for example, at the key geographic role to be played by Iran in China's One Belt One Road project.[17] At the same time, talk of closer military ties with Moscow and Beijing increases the geopolitical sensitivity of Iran in the eyes of Americans. At least, this is Iran's hope, which is why it plays the Russia and China card for the new Trump admin- istration to observe.

What is critical is to distinguish between Tehran's interest in military-to-military cooperation with states such as China and Russia for the sake of access to certain desired military hardware (such as the S-300 anti-air missiles) and as a way of lessening the perception of Iran as an isolated state against Tehran's reli- ance on either China or Russia as facilitators in shaping Tehran's latest military thinking. The ace in Iran's military capacity is still its ability to mobilize and wage war through local proxies in the Middle East, which is an ability that is fundamentally 'Iranian' in its make-up and hence does not require much foreign input from the likes of Russia or China.

5.   Wildcard: The Rouhani vs. IRGC fight

The rivalry between the elected government of Hassan Rou- hani and the generals of the IRGC is genuine and ongoing. It is de- batable whether this rivalry and competition for power have any meaningful impact on the Iranian military doctrine and Tehran's ambitions for the region, or whether Rouhani's views on a matter of strategic or military policy.

Many prominent Iranian academics do not think so. What mat-ters are only Khamenei's views, they say. For example, this be-low statement is from Kayhan Barzegar, an Iranian academic with very close ties to the Iranian regime:

> » Although Iran has a complicated political system and grants some independence to the president, particularly in domestic affairs, his ability in directing political change or making changes in the security policy of foreign affairs in contrast to the leader's [Khamenei] preference is, at most, trivial."[18]

It is interesting that Barzegar says that Rouhani's views on stra-tegic policies do not matter. What matters only are Khamenei's views. It might sound like a simple observation but this is an im-portant nuance that is often lost in Western capitals.

The entire eight-year effort by the Obama administration was to empower the Iranian 'moderates' against the 'hardliners' during his two-term presidency. However, Barzegar, a 'moderate' in the Iranian context, says that all significant geopolitical and military issues sit in the hands of Khamenei. Accordingly, the moderate versus hardliner split is not crucial at critical junctures in Iranian policy-making.

There are also signs that Khamenei is worried about the loy-alties of the Artesh, Iran's regular armed forces to the regime. Some of the last developments suggest this might be the case. Re-cently, a new group of leadership was introduced to take over the management of 'ideological-political' affairs in the Artesh. The new leadership was appointed by Mohammad Ali Al-e Hashem, Khamenei's top representative for 'ideological-political affairs' in the Artesh.

The job of these political managers is to brainwash the officers and to make sure that the leadership of the Artesh is loyal to the Islamic Republic (nezam) and Khamenei as the supreme leader. Al-e Hashem was appointed by Khamenei about seven years ago. Since his appointment, Al-e Hashem has hardly been a prominent figure. In fact, in the last seven years, Al-e Hashem has rarely been seen in the public domain.

There have been a few occasions when Al-e Hashem has com-mented about security risks to the regime. In November 2016, he said that following the 2015 nuclear deal 'America's plan is to ap-proach and infiltrate the pillars of the system.' Meanwhile, while he has always defended Iran's regional policies, it is only recently that Al-e Hashem and the ideological-political office have started to come out more forcefully in defense of Iran's military interven-tion in Syria.

It is not clear whether this development is linked to any signs of disillusionment inside the Artesh or whether the regime needs to show the face of Artesh as part of its controversial actions in Syr- ia. What is clear is that Ale-Hashem is highly trusted by Khamenei and that he is a 'fire-fighter' of sorts for the supreme leader. It has to be remembered that Khamenei appointed Ale-Hashem in July 2009 when a number of Artesh officers were arrested for plan- ning to show sympathy to Ayatollah Akbar Hashemi Rafsanjani during a Friday Prayer. In other words, Khamenei has deep trust in Ale-Hashem as his eyes in ears in one the most sensitive orga- nizations in Iran, the Artesh.[19]

Conclusion

The standard international assessment of the present Iranian military doctrine is that it is still inherently defensive. However, there is at the same time a broad recognition that Tehran has and continues to decentralize its military command. This is both to enhance its pursuit of 'hybrid warfare' – and above all strengthen Iran's flexibility to conduct asymmetric operations – but also as a result of an Iranian recognition of the superiority of the con- ventional forces of its key adversaries, most notably the United States.

The fact that the Pentagon was hugely successful in quickly dis- abling and destroying the command-and-control centers of its en- emies (in Iraq and Libya in particular) in recent conflicts is a real- ity that has been carefully noted by the Iranian military planners. Accordingly, the command-and-control in Iran is divided along 31 units based on the number of provinces in the country.

However, the Iranians do not appear to anticipate a conven- tional war with the United States in the foreseeable future. In- stead, and as has been pointed out above, at least the IRGC lead- ership appears to seriously experiment with the idea of a new 'forward-defense' that will enable Iran to maximize the advantag- es of asymmetric warfare.

It includes the use of rapid deployment of militias in conflict zones (such as by pro-Iran groups within Iraq's PMF Hashd Shaa- bi movement or Syria's National Defense Forces) and otherwise combines guerrilla tactics with massive information/media cam- paigns against Iran's rivals.

Whether the IRGC can continue to succeed in such efforts de- pends largely on two factors:

»   the willingness of Arab client groups to continue to be subservient to the IRGC agenda; and
»   the tolerance of the Iranian public to see the IRGC continue its military adventurism in the region despite the risks it brings.

In other words, the use of asymmetric warfare does not mean that Iran will not make use of its missiles or other conventional mil- itary capabilities, but rather that alongside taking advantage of them, the usage of asymmetric warfare tactics is also considered an advantage for the Islamic Republic, and it can increase defen- sive and offensive capabilities against enemies such as America.

Endnotes

(1) This was clearly expressed by various US military, intelligence and political figures at the high - level Aspen Security Forum (July 2017) where I was myself a participant. See http://aspensecurityforum.org

(2) For an example of background information on «hybrid warfare» see NATO's research on this topic: «Hybrid Warfare: Iranian and Russian Versions of Little Green Men and Contemporary Conflict». http://www.ndc.nato.int/news/news.php?icode=885

(3) The Gulf Military Balance (Vol.1). CSIS: https://www.csis.org/analysis/gulf - military - balance - volume – I

(4) For background, see «Immortal: A Military History of Iran and Its Armed Forces: Steven R. Ward (Pp. 77 - 273 and pp.326 - 313).

(5) What comes next for Iran's Defense Doctrine? (The National Interest: http:// nationalinterest.org/feature/what - comes - next - irans - defense - doctrine - 18360). For how the IRGC monitors this American debate about Iran's military doctrine, see Tasnim: http://bit.ly/2uGepq6

(6) See «Statement of General Joseph L. Votel on the posture of US Central Command» (http://www.centcom.mil/ABOUT - US/POSTURE - STATEMENT/).

(7) For tensions inside the Pentagon on the Iran question see «James Mattis 33 - year old grudge against Iran» (http://www.politico.com/magazine/story/12/2016/james - mattis - iran - secretary - of - defense - 214500).

(8) Syria: The Hidden Power of Iran (Joost Hilterman; the New York Review of Books) http://www.nybooks.com/daily/13/04/2017/syria - hidden - power - of - Iran/)

(9) For an extensive background discussion see Matt McInnis «Iranian Concepts of Warfare» (http://www.aei.org/publication/iranian - concepts - of - warfare - understanding - tehrans - evolving - military - doctrines/)

(10) See bio here: http://bit.ly/2oAamH3

(11) For the latest developments in the re - organization of Iranian regular armed forces, see «The establishment of 21 new offensive units in Artesh» (http://bit.ly/2vaOCcC)

(12) See Ali Saeedi's comments about the IRGC's intentions vis - à - vis troop deployment to Syria (http://donya - e - eqtesad.com/SiteKhan/1013573)

(13) Iran has been calling its missile program a «red line» for some time as a way of suggesting that it is «non - negotiable». See for example, «Iran calls missile program «red line». (http://en.isna.ir/news/93052814709/Iran - calls - missile - program - red - line).

(14) For context on Iran's relations with China and Russia see «The Authoritarian Resurgence: Iran Abroad. Journal of Democracy; April 2015).

(15) Iran and China conduct joint naval exercises in the Strait of Hormuz (https://www. rt.com/news/392837 - Iran - China - Hormuz - drills/)

(16) Shamkhani: Russia's use of Hamadan will continue (http://www.bbc.com/persian/ iran - 38942824)

(17) Thomas, Erdbrink. For China's Global Ambitions, Iran is at the Center of Everything». (New York Times, 25 July 2017) https://www.nytimes.com/25/07/2017/world/ middleeast/iran - china - business - ties.html

(18) Kayhan, Barzegar «Ayatollah Khamenei's Strategic Thinking» (Institute for Middle East Strategic Studies, Tehran) (http://en.cmess.ir/Default.aspx?tabid= 98&articleid=666&dnnprintmode=true&mid=477&SkinSrc=[G]Skins2%F_ default2%FNo+Skin&Container Src=[G]Containers2%F_default2%FNo+ Container)

(19) Al-Wefaq Online, official of ideological guidance: the army and the Revolutionary Guard taken the lead from enemies, http://cutt.us/9apOW

The Economic Activities of the Iranian Revolutionary Guards Corps (IRGC) Tools and Implications for Iran and the Region

Ahmad Shamsuddin Leila
An economist and a member of the editorial
board of the Journal for Iranian Studies

Introduction

Economic theory believes that the intervention of military institutions in the economic system undermines the functioning of this system. IRGC did not play a significant role in economic activity at the beginning of its era, but its military influence and political and religious support gave it gradual economic influence. Economic activities of IRGC ranged from the introduction of simple consumer goods to Tehran's markets to the establishment of airports, gas platforms, and oil wells to the possession of commercial companies and giant factories throughout the country—even to the possession of universities, newspapers, magazines, and publishing houses.

If IRGC is the reason behind the establishment of the state (as Khomeini stated), it seems understandable that it maintains a significant role within the state politically, militarily, and economically. IRGC maintains control over all matters within it. Khomeini, founder of the post-1979 state in Iran, described IRGC by saying, "If it weren't for IRGC, there would have been no state in Iran. I respect IRGC. And I love them. And I am always watching over them. They protected the nation when none was able to do so. And they are still assuming this role. They mirror the suffering of these people and its steadfastness on the battlefield across the history of the revolution."[1]

In 1979, the supreme leader Ayatollah Khomeini established IRGC as a revolutionary committee. Eventually, IRGC assumed its role of preserving the tenets of the revolution, imposing the pure ideology of Velayat-e Faqih by force, and resisting the forces opposing the revolution at home. Its role expanded to include defending the regime abroad and spreading its ideology in a bid to enforce the absolute rule of Velayat-e Faqih.[2] IRGC played a prominent role in the war with Iraq in the early 1980s; it gained the confidence of the regime and the religious authority and took the place of the regular army, which was gradually marginalized. Hence, the economic functions of IRGC grew after it gained the regime's confidence following the Iran-Iraq war.

IRGC began engaging in the country's economic affairs during the reign of President Hashemi Rafsanjani (1989-1997) by taking over small projects. After IRGC gained experience in business and the economy, it rivaled the government itself, exploiting its military and financial influence and supporting its religious leadership. Later, the military apparatus gained political leverage, combined with military and economic power and religious support. It has constantly sought a political influence that enhances its economic interests. Over the past ten years, a large part of the ownership of governmental corporations was transferred from state-owned companies to what the Iranians call the "semi-governmental sector" or the "cooperative sector." IRGC has boosted its economic influence through the privatization of state-run companies since the

1990s, after most of the stocks had been owned by the semi- governmental organizations through cooperatives associated with "revolutionary" institutions such as IRGC, Basij and the religious institutions of the supreme leader. During his presidency (2005- 2013), Ahmadinejad helped transfer 90 percent of ownership to the semi-governmental sector, unlike the other Iranian presidents, such as Rafsanjani (1989-1997) and Mohammad Khatami (1997-2005). The imposition of international sanctions on Iran – and the subsequent capital flight and suspension of international companies' activities – helped boost the contribution of Revolutionary Guard companies to all aspects of economic activity. Revolutionary Guard companies addressed production shortages and met consumer needs, especially in the fields of oil, gas, petrochemicals, and imports. This was especially the case considering the weakness of the Iranian government and the private sector and their inability to compete effectively. In other words, the noose was tightened around the private sector, creating more room for the companies of IRGC – in the presence of an Iranian president (Ahmadinejad) from within its ranks – to generate revenues that served the objectives and movements of the Guard both inside and outside Iran. Now, the largest economic contracts are conducted only through or with IRGC's consent.

When the nuclear agreement was signed in late 2015, the Revolutionary Guard's approval was a key factor in completing the agreement. If IRGC had not determined in advance how it would benefit from the deal, it would not have agreed to it. Under this agreement, IRGC would receive commissions from investment companies willing to work in the market. It would also see an increase in its financial revenues due to the re-exportation of oil, either from the government budget or IRGC companies' direct business in the energy sector, petrochemicals, and oil derivatives. In addition, IRGC companies would have new means of engaging in international trade through shell companies.

This study aims to uncover the aspects and nature of the economic activities of the Revolutionary Guard, both inside and outside the Iranian border, and analyze the implications for the economy, the Iranian citizen, and the Arab region through two main axes. The first axis deals with the economic strength of IRGC inside and outside Iran, such as investments inside Iran, the management of money and smuggling, the bazaar trade, IRGC's share of the government budget, and the political support it receives to consolidate economic power. This is in addition to revelations of ways in which the Guard used its military operations beyond Iran's borders, especially in Iraq and Syria, to maximize its economic interests. The second axis analyzes the implications that the IRGC's growing influence has for both the citizen and the Iranian economy and its relations abroad, along with repercussions for the Middle East. The conclusion states the study's proposed recommendations.

The Economic Activities of the Iranian Revolutionary
Guards Corps (IRGC) Tools and Implications for Iran and the Region

| 147

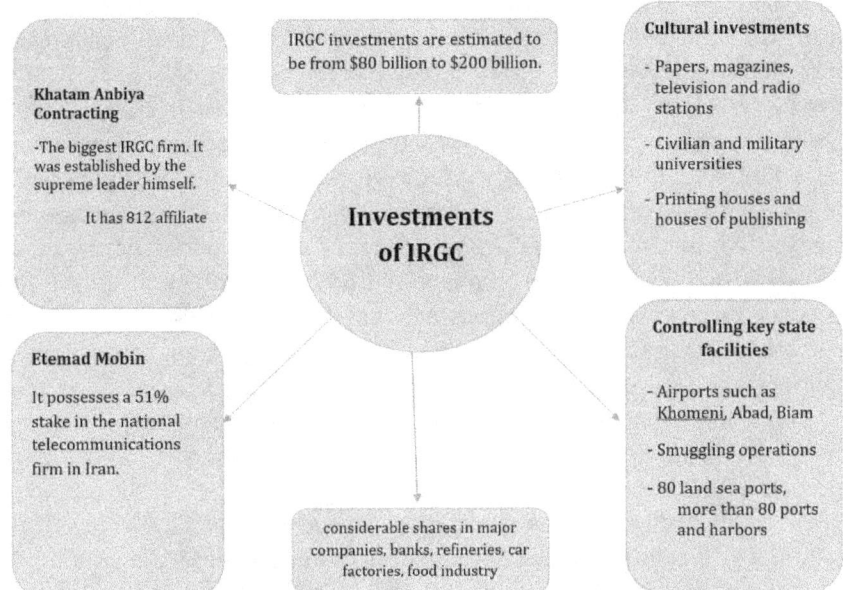

Investments of IRGC

IRGC investments are estimated to be from $80 billion to $200 billion.

Khatam Anbiya Contracting
- The biggest IRGC firm. It was established by the supreme leader himself.
It has 812 affiliate

Cultural investments
- Papers, magazines, television and radio stations
- Civilian and military universities
- Printing houses and houses of publishing

Etemad Mobin
It possesses a 51% stake in the national telecommunications firm in Iran.

Controlling key state facilities
- Airports such as Khomeni, Abad, Biam
- Smuggling operations
- 80 land sea ports, more than 80 ports and harbors

considerable shares in major companies, banks, refineries, car factories, food industry

Tools of IRGC's economic powers

The first axis deals with the internal and external tools affect- ing IRGC's financial resources and economic strength in various fields, including its extensive investments in Iran, money man- agement networks, and the bazaar trade; its increasing share of the government budget; and the political backing of its econom- ic strength. This is in addition to the external tools it uses, i.e., exploiting its military operations beyond Iran's borders to maximize its economic interests in some Arab countries.

First: Internal Tools

1. Many and various investments inside Iran

In Iran, IRGC operates oil and construction companies. It owns considerable shares in major companies, banks, refineries, car factories, petrochemical industry, metal industry, marine indus- try, tractor industry, iron and steel industry, pharmaceutical fac- tories, mills, drilling companies, and food industry.[3] As mentioned hereinbefore, while management and profits return to IRGC in secret. Therefore, the dominant apparatus is one of the largest investors in the main stock market in Tehran. Although there are no accurate statistics stating the size of IRGC's financial re- sources, various estimates from well-known institutions such as the Rand Corporation, and from American research institutions, point to tens of billions of dollars, with more than 500 companies in the Gulf, the Middle East, South East Asia, and Europe. Its an- nual profits are estimated at $5 billion. The final account of the Ministry of Finance in 2012 revealed that one institution (Khatam Anbiya and its affiliates) controlled 57% of the country's imports and 30% of its non-oil exports.[4] On the other hand, IRGC's control of airports and land, sea, and air borders has generated additional sources of income, from both the administration of these entities and the high fees that international airlines pay to use airports under the control of IRGC – such as the Khomeini International Airport,[5] Mehrabad Airport, and Biam Airport – for transporta- tion of goods in the capital, Tehran. IRGC also generates bulk rev- enues through illicit transactions, money smuggling/laundering, and controlling the movement of commodities and goods.

International and regional estimates differ as to the size of the contribution that Guard institutions make to the Iranian GDP. According to international estimates, IRGC directly control be- tween 20% and 40% of the Iranian economy.[6] Others estimate this amount as being 50% of the economy or production (GDP) of Iran.[7] IRGC's annual profit was estimated as being at least $5 billion.

With more than 500 companies operating in the Middle East, Southeast Asia and Europe, and until 2012 Khatam Al-Anbiya and its affiliated companies controlled 57% of the country's imports and 30% of its non-oil exports. [8]

2. Cases showing IRGC investments in the Iranian economy

The Khatam Anbiya Company for Engineering and Construction, one of the largest companies of IRGC, has at least 812 affiliated companies inside or outside Iran. Some estimates place the num- ber at 850 subsidiary companies, valued in the billions of dollars (2007).[9] The company was established by the founder of the Is- lamic Republic of Iran, Khomeini himself. Its economic influence has increased since the 1980s, after the Iran-Iraq war; it expand- ed in the construction sector until it became the largest contract- ing company in Iran. The company has received many of the coun- try's construction and reconstruction contracts, which involve multi-billion-dollar deals, to build roads, railways, dams, tunnels, and massive construction. The number of individuals employed in the company's projects is estimated at tens of thousands.[10]

Guard companies are large enough to require huge investments and to employ thousands of people. Etemad Mobin, a company run by IRGC, owns 51% of Iran's leading telecommunications company. The firm bought its stake in 2009 after the government had put Telecommunications Company for sale for $8 billion with- in a government privatization program. In addition to the tele-communications sector, Guard companies own 45% of the Bah- man Automotive Manufacturing Company (Mazda). The Guard's ownership has expanded to include mineral resources such as mines and quarries, including Anjouan, the largest zinc mine in the Middle East. IRGC also owns electronics, computrers and various means of communication production plants.[11] In addition to material investments, IRGC is engaged in several investments of a cultural nature, which reflect IRGC's economic clout, financial and political influence, and presence in the social lives of Iranians, achieved by spreading its tenets and doctrine via all means, with the aim of gaining the loyalty of the masses. In this area, IRGC's activity is evident. It issues specialized and qualitative magazines and papers such as Fars, Tasnim, and Raja news. It also possesses radio stations and printing houses for books, pamphlets, pictures, and posters. IRGC receives considerable attention on radio and television. In the field of education, it established a special univer- sity named the University of Al Hussein, which includes a number of faculty members in engineering, medicine, science, media, and political science, as well as academic faculty in military sciences such as Command and Staff, Chemical War, and the Officers Col- lege.[12]

3. Funds management and smuggling

IRGC indirectly controls the management of funds within Iran through its massive spread in the banking sector. Many private banks – unlike state-owned banks – in Iran are partly owned or managed by the political elites or IRGC. As a result of that control, officials[13] accuse IRGC of involvement in the smuggling of goods and money laundering,[14] using its influence and control over the country's banking and customs institutions and providing finan- cial facilities to smugglers.

IRGC manages a geographically and financially vast financial net- work. It boosts Iranians' loyalty to it by providing significant fi- nancial benefits through many of the country's informal financial institutions. It also provides low-interest bank loans and repay- ment facilities to individuals affiliated with its own organization.[15] IRGC has one of the largest financial networks in Iran, including the Mehr Economy, which owns hundreds of branches, as well as Al Ansar, Melli banks, and others, which it uses to attract Iranians' funds.[16] At the same time, these banks are used for money laun- dering when needed. IRGC's control of several entrances and exits in more than one airport in Iran and of about 80 ports and mari- nas (including some 40 in the southern province of Hormuzgan) is a direct result of IRGC's status as the main culprit involved in smuggling goods and distributing them inside Iranian markets and abroad in the Iranian bazaar. Former president Ahmadinejad was not embarrassed to describe the Revolutionary Guard com- manders explicitly as "smuggling brothers." Statistics relating the value of smuggled goods vary from country to country, but ac- cording to estimates, the value of smuggled goods was between $15 billion and

$25 billion annually between 2014 and 2016.[17] "If you want to get something from Iran without paying taxes, the Iranian Revolutionary Guard is the [entity] that will aid you [in doing] so, and there is no big businessman in Iran who works in- dependently of them or the government," Iranian analyst Mir Javedanfar told the Guardian newspaper.[18]

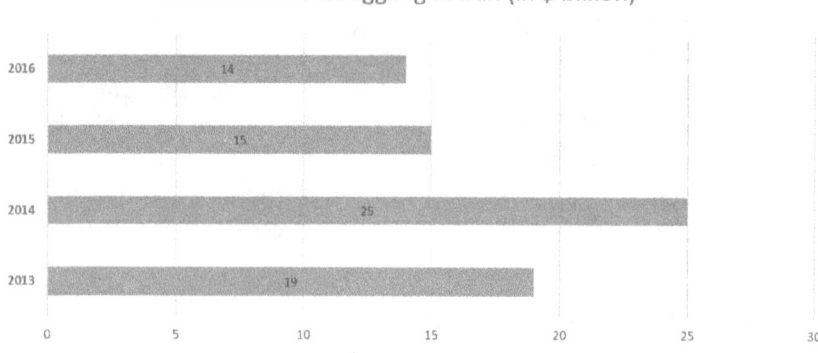

The volume of smuggling in Iran (in $ billion)

Source: Prepared by the researcher

Considering the above-mentioned tallies, it is not surprising that the Swiss Basel Institute for Governance put Iran at the top of a ranking of 146 countries that engaged in a list of crimes including money laundering and terrorist financing in 2017. This was the fourth time in a row that Iran received this designation, placing it ahead of North Korea and Afghanistan. No doubt, IRGC played a prominent role in placing Iran atop this blacklist. It controls the border crossings and owns several financial institutions, and thus maintains the elements required for smuggling and money laundering.

Table (1): The five most dangerous countries worldwide in the crimes of money laundering and terrorist financing from 2012- 2017

2012	2013	2014	2015	2016	2017
Iran	Afghanistan	Iran	Iran	Iran	Iran
Kenya	Iran	Afghanistan	Afghanistan	Afghanistan	Afghanistan
Cambodia	Cambodia	Cambodia	Tajikistan	Tajikistan	Guinea-Bissau
Haiti	Tajikistan	Tajikistan	Guinea-Bissau	Uganda	Tajikistan
Tajikistan	Iraq	Guinea-Bissau	Mali	Guinea-Bissau	Laos

Source: Bezel Indicator for money laundering and terror financing for 2017

4. Bazaar trade

Before the relationship between the Revolutionary Guard and the bazaar is explained, a brief description of the bazaar and its role in supporting the economic strength of the Revolutionary Guard should be given. "Bazaar" is a Persian word that refers to a big market where business activities such as selling and buying take place. The bazaar consists of hundreds of adjacent shops in all major Iranian cities, such as Tehran, Isfahan, Kerman, Tabriz, and Qazvin. The most famous is the Tehran bazaar. Historically, the bazaar has played an active role in political life inside Iran. Its institution is characterized by independence and by the desire to maximize its commercial interests, at times aligning with the religious establishment or the ruling authority as necessary. The bazaar includes hundreds of thousands of shopkeepers whose in- fluence extends beyond the control of the bazaar's workers and assistants. It transcends thousands of street vendors, retailers, and small brokers, and reaches the countryside, where hundreds of thousands of small factories for carpeting, footwear, furniture, and commercial farms are financed by wealthy businessmen and traders in cities. A close and historical relationship exists between the merchants and the religious establishment based in Iran (i.e., the owner of the upper hand in decision making). The bazaar, with all its merchants and craftsmen, is the main financier of the religious establishment through Zakat and Khoms in the Shiite Twelver doctrine. According to this understanding, the share of the Prophet's Family is 20% of the merchants' profits. They are spent on the channels by Sharia.

The bazaar played a prominent role in supporting the clerics' rev- olution in Iran in February 1979 and earlier. During the revolu- tion, Bazaar merchants and clerics organized about two-thirds of the marches and demonstrations in the streets of various Iranian cities. Initially, they also offered financial support to achieve the aims of the revolution. After the success of the revolution, the ma- jor bazaar merchants assumed important political and economic positions in the state. Some became ministers and parliamentar- ians; some became the heads of major newspapers. Among the latter was iron merchant Hussein Mehdian, who headed Kayhan newspaper. After heightened economic activity in the nineties, traders entered the bazaar and split it into two main classes. One class consisted of traders who supported the Iranian revolution financially in 1979, thereby gaining the confidence of the system after the revolution and supporting its positions politically. The scope of their work was mainly in imports and distribution. The second class consisted of IRGC merchants who had been compet- ing with bazaars in the field of imports and distribution, seek- ing to increase IRGC's financial resources and taking advantage of the control of ports and border crossings. This allowed them to smuggle goods without paying customs duties and, thereby, to increase profits. The existence of the two main classes of mer- chants – lower and middle – led to feelings that the merchants were unfairly treated, with no political base of support to protect their interests. Consequently, they organized several protests.

5. IRGC's share of the budget

IRGC's resources are not limited to its own investments and re- sources. It has an annualized share of the government budget. The size of the annual budget allocated to IRGC varies according to the orientation of the leaders and their closeness to one of the competing camps in the Iranian political system – either the fun- damentalist stream or the reformist stream. Of course, this bud- get does not include the total financial resources available to IRGC. However, when we review the share that the powerful mili- tary body received from the government budget in recent years, we find that it continued to rise even in the presence of a presi- dent affiliated with the reformist movement. In the last year of Ahmadinejad's rule, the government's budget allocated to IRGC an amount more than double the budget allocated to the coun- try's official army. IRGC's budget was about $3.3 billion in 2014, while the military budget was only $1.5 billion. When the reform- ist president, Hassan Rouhani, tried to increase the army's budget so that it approached IRGC's budget, he failed in reducing the gap. The army's share increased to $1.75 billion in the 2016 budget while IRGC's share fell to $4.1 billion from $5 billion in 2015.[19] At- tempts to reduce the influence of IRGC did not last long; its pow- ers and clout overshadowed those of the president himself, as well as those of the president of the Iranian parliament, which passes or suspends a former member of IRGC. Therefore, the Guard's allocation in the 2017 budget increased by 80% com- pared to its allocation in the 2016 budget, reaching $7.4 billion.[20] This meant that IRGC's share of the budget was twice that of the army's.

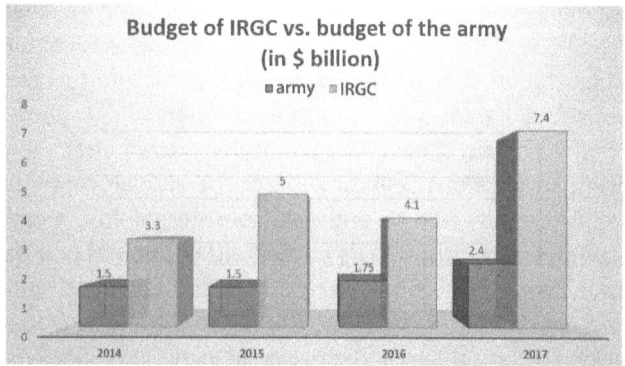

The Economic Activities of the Iranian Revolutionary
Guards Corps (IRGC) Tools and Implications for Iran and the Region
| 153

Political support for IRGC as a source of economic strength

Since its inception, the existence of IRGC has been linked to the support of political leaders, from the first leadership of the coun- try (represented by the leader of the revolution), to a political authority that changes every four years, and even to the appoint- ment of former leaders of the Guard as the heads of the country's judicial and regulatory authorities. The support of the political authority may vary according to the directions each president takes, but there is always a minimum of support for IRGC – or, in other words, a ceiling for criticism of it by the political authority. Ahmadinejad's presidency (2005-2013) was the golden period of harmony between the Revolutionary Guard and the political au- thority. President Ahmadinejad was himself a general within the Iranian Revolutionary Guard before he assumed the presidency and being mayor of Tehran from 2002 to 2005. During this period, Ahmadinejad granted facilities to companies belonging to IRGC in Tehran, allowing them – in particular, the contracting companies Khatam Anbiya and Khatam Awsia – to carry out economic ac- tivities. After Ahmadinejad became president, he appointed the head of the Khatam Anbiya Foundation, Rustam Qasimi, to the po- sition of oil minister, a role Qasimi held from 2011 to 2017. Such a move allowed the Guard to take advantage of this vital sector in the country.

IRGC has asserted its economic influence by acquiring as many executive and political positions in Iran as possible. An increasing number of its members serve as deputies in the Iranian parlia- ment (about 70 to 80 deputies in the 7th session of the Iranian Parliament, 2004-2008) and as members of the municipal coun- cils. IRGC's members are appointed ministers and deputy minis- ters in the government, and governors in the various provinces. Also, its military is double that of the regular army. The govern- ment gave lucrative projects to IRGC's construction companies at the expense of the private sector in the areas of oil and gas, roads, reconstruction, publishing, and information; in addition, it increased the import and distribution of goods and commod- ities smuggled into Iran during the period when sanctions were in place.[21] IRGC returned the favor to Ahmadinejad by repressing the protests of 2009, which broke out over the suspected elector- al fraud (press interview of the former IRGC chief Hussein Ham- dani with an Iranian magazine in 2015).[22]

Although Ahmadinejad has been removed from power, there are many like him in senior positions throughout the country – people who provide political support for IRGC and, in some cases, offer legal coverage. The head of the highest supervisory body in any political system, the parliament, was a former member of IRGC. Ali Larijani, head of Iran's parliament, describes IRGC – not the army – as "the strongest force in the region, and that is why no en- emy dares to attack Iran." How can he merely criticize his monop- oly and competition for the public and private sectors, subjecting his companies to the same things to which private companies are subject: fees and taxes?

Ali Shamkhani, one of the founders of IRGC, who served as defense minister, is secretary of the Supreme National Security Council. The achievement of internal and external national security objec- tives (including the spread of Shiism and foreign military inter- ventions from the Iranian point of view and in accordance with the Iranian constitution) requires considerable financial resourc- es. Thus, the Guard receives the green light for economic expan- sion to achieve those goals.

Second: The External Tools

The economic exploitation of military influence beyond borders

The Iranian constitution states that the role of IRGC is not limited to protecting the borders, but rather is to spread the provisions of Islamic law throughout the world via Jihad (Article 8 of the Irani- an Constitution of 1985, page 12). Article 154 of the Constitution states that "Iran has the right to protect the legitimate struggle of the oppressed against the arrogant at any point in the world, while at the same time not interfering in the internal affairs of other peoples" (Iranian Constitution, 1985, p. 97).[23] An obvious contradiction exists between what Iran is doing to "protect the struggle of the oppressed" and non-interference in the internal affairs of other people.

For decades, IRGC has cost billions – or even hundreds of billions– of dollars due to its foreign meddling and support for military organizations beyond borders. Some estimate the cost of Iran's involvement in regional and international conflicts since the 1979 Iranian Revolution to be $3,000 billion (i.e., $3 trillion)[24] – an amount higher than the United Kingdom's GDP in 2016. These organizations or their affiliated states still have a price to pay, not only in political and sectarian dependency but also a material cost. The Iranian project in the region reaps commercial and economic revenues along with security or sectarian gains. IRGC's name has been synonymous with the support and funding of many non- state military actors in the form of training or supplying weap- ons, troops, and equipment. Such is the case with the Lebanese Hezbollah and Popular Mobilization Forces in Iraq, Houthi mili- tias in Yemen, and the pro-regime militias in Syria. After the fall of the regime of former Iraqi President Saddam Hussein, IRGC's role in the region expanded; it increased its support for Bashar Assad and Houthis in Yemen at the beginning of the Arab Spring revolutions.[25]

The Economic Activities of the Iranian Revolutionary
Guards Corps (IRGC) Tools and Implications for Iran and the Region

|155

Iran's gains from military intervention beyond borders

Iraq and Iran are the second and third largest producers, respec- tively, of crude oil in the Organization of Petroleum Exporting Countries (OPEC). The combined production of both countries is equal to the production of Saudi Arabia, the largest producer in the organization. Iran's domination of Iraq's security has led to the imposition of an Iranian vision or consensus with respect to the size and production plans and an influence on the world oil supply – and, thus, its global prices – in a manner that may contra- dict the plans and objectives of the other members of OPEC. The organization already failed to reach a unified decision to reduce production when prices fell to record levels between mid-2014 and late 2016. Iran's refusal to reduce production levels was the primary factor in this lack of a unified agreement – sometimes accompanied by Iraqi support.[26] Iraq is ranked as the second larg- est export destination for Iran. The volume of trade exchange be- tween Iraq and Iran was over $6 billion in 2016 – and $13 billion in the same year if one adds the oil trade and the sale of electric- ity.[27] Although no accurate information is available about the size of IRGC trade in Iraq, it is not unlikely that IRGC, as the Iranian major player in Iraq, maintains a significant share of trade be- tween the two countries, and controlling at least 30% of non-oil exports in Iran.

On the other hand, Syria comes in second in terms of the econom- ic gains of IRGC or Iran in general. In Syria, Iran obtained a license to operate the mobile phone system, following the signing of part- nership documents between Tehran and Damascus during the visit of Syrian Prime Minister Emad Khamis to Iran in December 2016. It also obtained the right to extract and transfer phosphate in the eastern region of Syria (50 km south of the Syrian city of Palmyra); in addition, thousands of hectares of agricultural land were handed over to Iranian companies to raise livestock, while Iran seized 5,000 hectares of land to establish Iranian oil tanks and stations.[28] In his letter on "Ways of Financing IRGC," Shaykh Turku, a doctoral student at Cairo University, sees IRGC investing in Iran so professionally that it does not show any effect on the entity, while investments in the media are reportedly carried out through chambers of commerce, businessmen, and private inves- tors. He also confirms that the loans the Iranian regime gave to Syria to face the losses of war were in exchange for Syrian market access, received by dozens of Iranian companies.[29]

The repercussions that IRGC's economic
incursion has on Iran and the region

IRGC's control of the Iranian economy has led to many negative repercussions for both citizens and the local economy in terms of Iran's relationship with the outside world on the one hand, and the security and stability of the region on the other hand. We shall discuss these implications in detail:

» **Losing alternative development opportunities for the Iranian people and development sectors:** Perhaps the most critical and dangerous effect of IRGC's control of significant financial and economic resources in Iran is the channeling of those resources to the war machine rather than their use in improving citizens' lives, especially given the poor quality of life in Iran and the modest economic and social indicators there. Even though Iran is a rich nation, between 10 million and 12 million Iranians live in absolute poverty (i.e., do not earn an income that meets their basic needs). These people deserve the billions of dollars spent annually on armed operations outside the Iranian border. If these funds were employed across the various government agencies, they would have a positive impact on the areas of training and employment, consequently raising standards of living and upgrading sectors that push development, such as education, health, infrastructure, and private investment. On the other hand, the meddling of a military institution such as IRGC in commercial and investment business is economically harmful and destroys the private sector. Most of the work is done by recruits who do not receive salaries or who receive minimal payment. This reduces the cost of workforce for IRGC, and the private sector cannot compete. The private sector is typically the force behind creativity and evolution in any economy.

» **Threatening the country's monetary and financial policy:** The mismanagement committed by some of IRGC's credit institutions (especially non-banking ones), which offer significant financial benefits until they go bankrupt, threatens to prevent the achievement of the central bank's monetary policy objectives of maintaining price levels and investing in the economy. It also threatens to create a financial crisis in the country if credit remains available. On the other hand, through its non-economic behavior, IRGC impedes the achievement of the objectives of the state's fiscal policy, as IRGC is involved in smuggling operations that drain the state treasury of major resources, including duties and taxes (the primary source of revenue for the Iranian government). It seems that no entity in Iran will be able to stop IRGC. The Iranian president himself could not directly charge IRGC with involvement in smuggling, but only hinted at it in separate statements. In one of them, he said, "There is [a] corrupt body behind the smuggling of goods, and we must address this corruption."[30]

*The Economic Activities of the Iranian Revolutionary
Guards Corps (IRGC) Tools and Implications for Iran and the Region*

|157

» **Curtailing the most significant gains of the nuclear deal and fighting against domestic and foreign investments:** The Rouhani government, or the government of measure and hope, relied heavily on foreign partnerships after the nuclear deal to save the Iranian economy from the years of recession it experienced during the prolonged economic blockade. However, IRGC's meddling in the local economy makes foreign investors very cautious about working with Iranian companies. IRGC companies are included on an international blacklist, and foreign companies that cooperate with them face legal penalties and fines. In addition, while many Iranian companies are publicly represented as private sector companies owned by private individuals, a search of their ownership structures reveals links to companies or individuals in IRGC who have been hit by international sanctions or who are on the US Treasury Department's Office of Foreign Assets Control sanctions list. Therefore, any international investment not calculated with Iranian companies could face substantial fines and prohibitions against dealing with US companies. IRGC is hampering local investment, with the Iranian private company Bishkaman Kowar Yazd being the best case in point. The company had the best chance to buy a %51 stake in Iran Telecom when it was privatized in 2009, but it had to compete with two companies that, while having no experience in the field, were affiliated with IRGC. The two firms were Tawseat Etemad and Shahryar Mehstan.[31] One day before the results of the purchase bid were declared, the firm was driven out of the bidding process under the pretense that it lacked security requirements. IRGC won the tender, worth 8$ billion. The tender was tailored to give IRGC the biggest deal in the annals of Iranian stocks, with the rival firm forcibly driven out of the purchase bid.

The foreign investor is afraid to exist in an investment climate in which a state organization imposes on economic and commercial activities; the investor fears that he may lose his investments directly or indirectly through his forcible removal from an investment opportunity in favor of the state. He may also be exposed to manipulation and abuse of power, as was the case with the sale of the Iranian telecommunications company. Iran's ranking in the Business Performance Index 2018 was 124, down from 118 in 2016. The index measures the ease or difficulty of creating businesses, using several sub-indicators such as the time required to create and end a new business, the time and cost required to end business disputes, and other indicators that measure the ease or difficulty of doing business.

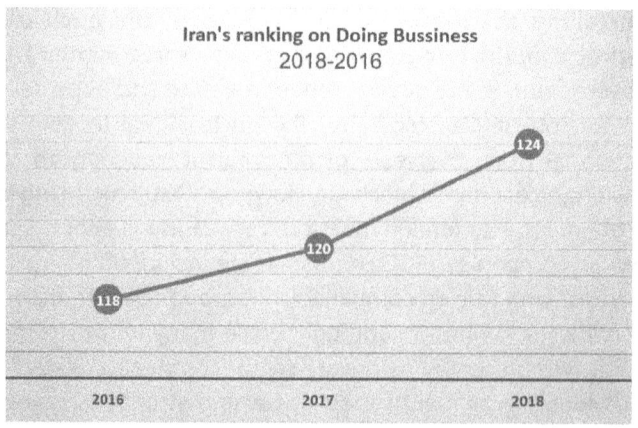

Source: Transparency International

» **Bankruptcy of private sector firms and increasing unemployment**

The presence of the Revolutionary Guard on the map of import- ers of goods and commodities in Iran, through its control of many of the country's customs outlets, creates unfair competitive ad- vantages among local producers if those goods are imported into the country without tariffs. In addition, foreign companies must pay various production taxes and expenditures. This results in re- duced competitiveness, fewer sales, the accumulating of goods in warehouses, or – if worst comes to worst – the closure of facto- ries, the laying off of workers, an increase in unemployment, and a lack of production, which in turn could lead to higher levels of inflation.

» **Lack of transparency and lost confidence in the Iranian economy**

IRGC's control of key sectors of Iran's economy, such as energy, petrochemicals, banking, insurance, contracting and commerce prevents competition in these sectors and causes the investor to lose confidence in the system's ability to create a free and honest trade competition. Revolutionary Guard companies are exempt from most of the costs incurred by domestic or foreign investors, including taxes, legal fees, and even illegal costs such as gratuities and gifts. IRGC is sufficient to facilitate any deal or business.

The Economic Activities of the Iranian Revolutionary
Guards Corps (IRGC) Tools and Implications for Iran and the Region

|159

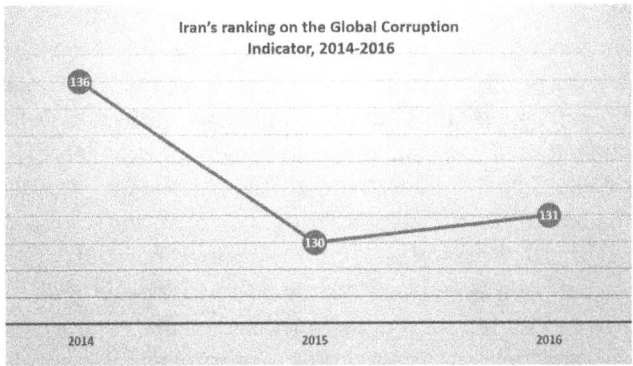

Source: The researcher data according to Transparency International

Confidence in the integrity and transparency of any economy is an important factor in attracting foreign investment or expelling it from any economy. Two annual international indexes measure the degree of corruption or lack of transparency, as well as the ease of doing business. Iran is ranked low on both indexes.

In 2016, Iran ranked 131 out of 176 countries on Transparency International's Corruption Perceptions Index – an arrangement equating Iran with Kazakhstan and Nepal, and behind Togo and Pakistan, for example, Scandinavia, Sweden, Norway, and Finland. In 2015, Iran's ranking in the list fell from 136 to 130, then rose again in 2016.[32] This indicator reveals the degree of institutional and governmental corruption and the use of judicial authority in conflict resolution.

» **The destabilization of the Middle East region**

Increasing the financial resources and economic strength of IRGC, both internal and external, increases its military influence and in- terventions in the Middle East to achieve its political and sectar- ian goals while protecting its economic projects in Iraq and Syria and creating new interests in Yemen and Lebanon. No doubt, this expansion will lead to more tensions and conflicts in the region, feeding sectarian conflicts between countries – or within the same state – and threatening the stability of the Gulf states and the security of their citizens through terrorist groups (such as the Houthi group in Yemen) supported by IRGC. IRGC is providing them with money and dangerous weapons that have more than once fired ballistic missiles from Yemeni territory onto the Saudi capital of Riyadh.

The cost of reconstructing Iraq and Syria will reach tens of bil- lions of dollars over years of construction. The Iraqi city of Mo- sul alone needs investments of nearly $100 billion to repair what warfare has damaged, including buildings, roads, bridges, and ed- ucational, health, and administrative institutions. Iran will play a significant role in the reconstruction and rehabilitation of the in- frastructure. The company Khatam Anbiya will play a role in con- tracting. Meanwhile, post-war investment in the field of medicine and medical equipment will be a promising opportunity upon the return of displaced persons and war casualties to their cities, and the return of Iraqi immigrants to Iran during the years of war. In 2017, as many as 200,000 Iraqi therapeutic tourists in Iran sought hospitalization.[33] In Syria, the Khatam Anbiya company is already operating and is seeking to export electricity from Iran to Syria and Lebanon after connecting it to a network; it is also seeking to win as many Syrian reconstruction deals as possible.[34] In the end, Iran must be rewarded for supporting the Syrian regime and receive compensation for its material and human losses in one form or another.

It is certain that IRGC's companies, especially those specializing in construction and contracting, will play a vital role over the next several years in the reconstruction of Arab cities destroyed after the end of ISIS and the defeats of the armed opposition. The urgent need for reconstruction may prompt the governments of some countries to accept Iranian conditions or grant concessions in return for soft investments after the war has exhausted the re- sources of their governments. The Iranian commercial mentality instinctively will not pass up these opportunities without taking the lion's share of investment reconstruction opportunities in the two countries – especially in light of the Iranian economy's need to impose its own will and vision on the future of the region and the ruling political systems and their relations with neighboring Arab and Gulf countries.

Conclusion

IRGC has transcended the tasks outlined during the Khomeini era that began in 1979; it now plays the roles of government and the private sector in Iran. A small independent economic entity that began in the 1980s was developed and supported by political and religious leaders in the 1990s. IRGC expanded its economic activi- ties role in the first decade of the millennium, especially during the two terms of Ahmadinejad's presidency. Despite his efforts, Iran's current president, Hassan Rouhani, could not trim the substantial economic empire's clout. This is because IRGC maintains various financial sources fed by investments within Iran, including indus- try, construction, and banks, whether legal or illegal, along with an annual share of a growing government budget. All this is add- ed to political support from the Iranian state's decision-making circles, such as parliament. In addition to the internal financial resources, IRGC maintains projects in places of military influence outside Iranian borders, such as Iraq and Syria, to name but a few. This guarantees the recovery of even a small portion of the vast sums spent outside the nation's borders.

The Economic Activities of the Iranian Revolutionary
Guards Corps (IRGC) Tools and Implications for Iran and the Region

|161

Iran's decision-makers ignore the grave repercussions of IRGC's economic actions, which harm citizens, the business environment, and real economic competition, saying that IRGC activities are for the good of both sides. It may be true in the operation or supply of some commodities, but it creates economic repercussions, such as threats to the financial and monetary policy of the country, the bankruptcy of private sector companies, the undermining of the most important gains of the nuclear agreement with Iran (i.e., at- tracting foreign investment to the Iranian market), an increase in annual spending on armed interventions outside the border to eliminate development opportunities for the Iranian economy and people, the destabilization of Arab states and the threaten- ing of their citizens' security, and the fomenting of sectarian strife within and between them and their neighbors. The decision-mak- er in Iran must be aware that, because of the previously explained negative repercussions for both the economy and the Iranian citi- zen, the role of military institutions should not transcend internal security tasks to include economic tasks.

The Iranian decision-maker must realize that advanced econ- omies succeed in assuming a global position not because they operate in a resistance economy, but because their economy is specialized and cooperates with the world. Iran must enhance the quality of its products and export them to all countries of the world; otherwise, its economy will collapse and perish. Econo- mies, depending on their own strengths and by cooperating with the outside world, can tackle their weaknesses and concentrate their efforts on investing resources at home instead of squander- ing them abroad.

Endnotes

(1) «Iranian Revolutionary Guard and its Role in Exporting the Revolution." Iranian Anthology Magazine, January 24,2005.

(2) In brief, Velayat-e Faqih means that the supreme leader is the deputy of the Absent Imam. He then shall have an absolute authority over all institutions. He is immune to accountability or dismissal. He has an authority that supersedes the powers of the state apparatuses because he is simply the representative of Imam Mahdi, Messiah, who has been in occultation for 1400 years, according to the Shiite doctrine.

(3) Saud, Zahid. "Iranian Economy at the Mercy of IRGC' Mafia." Al-Arabiya.net. February 2016,4. Accessed October 2017,17. https://goo.gl/ru8lvb.

(4) Aisha, Al-Suwaidi, "Ahmadinejad, the Revolutionary Guard and Chess Pieces." Middle East Online. 2012. Accessed October 2017,17. https://goo.gl/sxbqSh.

(5) «Who Controls the Iranian Economy?" Voice of Germany Radio. February 2016,22. Accessed October 2017,18. https://goo.gl/W3qyC9

(6) Iran's GDP reached about 412$ billion in 2017.

(7) Paolo, Magri, and Annalisa, Perteghella. Iran after the Deal: The Road Ahead. Milano: ISPI, 2015. Accessed October 2017,10. https://goo.gl/CVTF9N.

(8) Aisha, Al-Suwaidi, op. cit.

(9) Ahmad, Shamsuddin. The Future of Iran's Economy after the Lifting of International Sanctions. Arabian Gulf Centre for Iranian Studies. May 2016,25. Accessed October,19 2017. https://goo.gl/74trAk.

(10) Ali Nada, Anbaa'. "Iran ... Economic Penetration of the Revolutionary Guard Shakes Off Foreign Investment." May 2016,31. Accessed October 2017,21. https://goo.gl/dt95PS.

(11) Mark, Gregory. "Expanding Business Empire of IRGC." BBC. July 2010,26. Accessed October 2017,22. https://goo.gl/8Znixp.

(12) Iranian Revolutionary Guard and its Role in Exporting the Revolution." Iranian Anthology Magazine, January 25,2005.

(13) Ali Hashemi Rafsanjani acted as the former Iranian president and former president of the Expediency Discernment Council.

(14) Money laundering is carried out by conferring legal cover on funds generated from illegitimate sources. This happens when the funds are traded in the official banking system.

(15) Iran: The Rise of IRGC' Financial Empire; How the Supreme Leader and IRGC Rob the People to Fund International Terror. National Council of Resistance of Iran - U.S. Representative Office. 9,2017.

(16) Gregory, Mark. IDEM.

(17) "Parliamentary Assembly: Three Thousand Containers a Day, Smuggled Goods to Iran." Radio Farda. March 2016,29. http://cutt.us/OvQhP.

(18) "The Financial Power of IRGC." The Guardian. February 2010,10. Accessed February 2018,14. https://goo.gl/Hx2Vg9.

(19) Mutasim, Siddiq. "Military Institutions between Trust and Marginalization: A Comparison between the Status of the Revolutionary Guard and the Army in the Structure of the Iranian Regime." Journal of Iranian Studies 1, no. 1 (December: (2016 145.

(20) Saeed, Ghasseminejad. Iran's Revolutionary Guard Gets a Raise. Foundation for Defense of Democracies. April 2017,3. Accessed 12 March 2018. https://goo.gl/UGmtCA.

(21) Yousef, Azizi. Bazaar and the Iranian Regime: The Dialectics of Economy and Politics. Arabian Gulf Centre for Iranian Studies. April 2016,30. Accessed October 2017,30. https://goo.gl/Qy9uJm.

(22) Farzaneh, Rustayi. Conspiracy Theory of Spearheaded by IRGC, Ibrahim Rasi. Arabian Gulf Center for Iranian Studies. April 2017,18. Accessed October 2017,29. https://goo. gl/c2bPmF.

(23) Islamic Republic of Iran. Ministry of Islamic Guidance. Constitution of the Islamic Republic of Iran. Tehran, 1403 AH.

(24) Shatha, Khalil. Iran's Expanded Agenda: Its Economy Is Diluted, Middle East Stability Struggles. Center for Strategic Studies and Research. January 2017,14. Accessed November 2017,2. https://goo.gl/x4Si4S.

(25) Dan, Galgir. "Iranian Revolutionary Guard, History of the Selected Military Organization, KSA." Journal for Iranian Studies, Arabian Gulf Centre for Iranian Studies. March 151: 2017.

(26) In November 2016, an agreement was reached to reduce the volume of oil production except for in Iran, which increased its production to levels achieved before the imposition of the oil embargo and then froze production at it.

(27) "Volume of Trade Exchange Between Iran and Iraq Amounts to 13$ Billion Annually." Al-Wefaq Online. November 2016. Accessed November 2017,3. https://goo.gl/mcTSH7.

(28) "Assignment of Mobile Phone and 'Dairy' Network Points to Iran During Syria's Prime Minister's Visit." Radio Farda. 2016. http://cutt.us/LgW0R.

(29) Walid, Abulkheir. "Iranian Revolutionary Guard Seeks Economic Control of Syria." Diarna. December 2016,12. Accessed December 2017,20. https://goo.gl/bmvuqw.

(30) Mutasim, Siddiq, Op. Cit.: 145.

(31) Saud, Zahid, Op. Cit.

(32) Transparency International. "Corruption Perception Index 2016." Accessed November 2017,20. www.transparency.org.

(33) Amran, Emrouz. "Iran's Economic Profit from ISIL's Defeat." http://soo.gd/OUmw.

(34) Bozorgmehr, Sharafedin, and Francis, Ellen. "IRGC Reap Economic Gains in Syria." Reuters. January 2017,19. Accessed November 2017,25. https://goo.gl/zsGLUj.

Closure

As Ali Khamenei has maintained the political and religious au- thority in Iran for over 27 years, his popularity has declined. Meanwhile, his dependence on the Iranian military, especially the Revolutionary Guard, has increased and become a tool for con- trolling internal affairs and the main pillar of political balance. On the other hand, the Iranian presidency refuses to deal with the IRGC as a political faction, or as a military institution with super- visory powers over the performance of the government. It rejects the hegemony of the IRGC over the Iranian economy. This situa- tion represents a real crisis currently facing the Iranian regime at the domestic level. Iran's future depends on the outcome of this conflict.

The military, with the first part of the Iranian regime, the institu- tion of the Supreme Leader, is in a state of consensus. This serious split of the two parties (the military and the political system) into four parties (the Institution of the Supreme Leader, the Presiden- cy, the Army, and IRGC) predicts a clash if one of the parties is ab- sent. However, the explosion is expected to result in the aftermath of Ali Khamenei's death, who, for the long duration of his tenure, unified his personal position and the Supreme Leader position, not identifying his deputy or successor. On the other hand, this situation excludes the third party – the Iranian people, who are not satisfied with corrupt democratic practices, such as a series of presidential, parliamentary, local, and other elections that no longer distract Iranians from the core of the struggle for power in Iran. Ali Khamenei and the IRGC have become a radical force that draws Iran into an era of revolutionary practices, prevent- ing it from opening up to the outside world in accordance with the values of international cooperation and the principle of being a good neighbor in the region. Revolutionary ideological values continue to govern IRGC's view of the outside world. Khamenei supports this trend due to his personality and experience, which were formed during the periods of revolution and the war with Iraq. He discards any rejection of his policies – for instance, the attacks expressed by the former late President Hashemi Rafsan- jani, who said that this is the era of talks, not the era of missiles.

At the external level, the military has become one of the most important players in Iran's foreign policy. The military and IRGC for- mulate international cooperation policies, appoint ambassadors, discuss international agreements, send the regime's messages to the outside world through weapons and military manufacturing programs, and determine the extent to which missiles are used to serve Iran's political objectives. In Iran, missiles have become a more important foreign policy tool than the diplomatic appara- tus. Through policies of Shiite militarization, the military seeks to place Shiites around the world under its umbrella and turn them into armed military elements. This undermines the national con- cept in a number of neighboring countries. It overthrows the po- litical balance by militarizing Shiites in these countries, enabling them to achieve a greater political role in their nations. The result is that these countries become politically and economically de- pendent on Iran.

The Iranian military seeks to clone the Revolutionary Guards and disseminate the guerilla model. One of the IRGC's military doc- trine objectives is to clone and build military and paramilitary cluster institutions in those countries in turmoil, consistent with the Iranian military in terms of organization and sectarianism.

The IRGC plays the role of unofficial militias and participates in the tactics of terrorist organizations. Iran's support of terrorism is closely linked to its objectives. Observation of the Iranian situ- ation over the past 38 years – the age of the Iranian regime – has shown that a direct-armed clash against it will create more ex- tremism and internal and external violence. This would give the Iranian regime greater national cohesion and deepen the wide- spread feeling that support for the regime is necessary regardless of the status of public freedoms and the condition of civil society. At the same time, the feeling that no threat exists would provoke the desire to expand and gain areas of influence and elements of power. This type of historical military approach dominates the Iranian political decision-maker; therefore, the confrontation of the ideology of the Iranian military must be continued non-mili- tarily through the beginning of an international campaign against it, without the involvement of the regime's other sections. Accord- ingly, this could prove that Iran has integrated the military struc- ture legally although its actual practice is illegal and it is involved in illegal acts and activities. Thus, there is no difference between the IRGC and Al-Qaeda and ISIS, except that the IRGC carries out its activities under the cloak of the Iranian state. As the Irani- an military doctrine is based on the model of guerrilla warfare, it may wage a model war through the economy. Therefore, it is crucial to build a counter-military doctrine based on non-mili- tary confrontation to paralyze the Iranian military's capabilities and effectiveness, as well as to provide a model of development, prosperity, and growing levels of freedom. This would deprive the Iranian military of the presence of the enemy, which promotes the survival and continuity of its role.

In conclusion, this book resulted from the Military Institution in Iran between Revolution and Statehood workshop which attempt- ed to discover the Iranian military's aspects and dimensions at the levels of ideology, military activities, its engagement with the political system, external expansion, economic work, and effort. The findings will be added to previous research into the Iranian issue as preparation for future efforts.

Iran Supreme Leadership
Usurped Power

Shiite Political Controversy Between
Arab and Iranian Religious Authorities

RASANAH
المعهد الدولي للدراسات الإيرانية
International Institute for Iranian Studies

www.rasanah-iiis.org

@rasanahiiis @Rasanahiiis rasanahiiis Info@rasanahiiis.com

CPSIA information can be obtained
at www.ICGtesting.com
Printed in the USA
BVHW031812230221
600777BV00016B/209